2

AF843875

GLOBAL RECESSION - CAUSES, IMPACTS AND REMEDIES

LABOR MARKET RECOVERY AFTER THE RECESSION OF 2007-2009

SELECT ANALYSES

Global Recession - Causes, Impacts and Remedies

Additional books in this series can be found on Nova's website under the Series tab.

Additional e-books in this series can be found on Nova's website under the e-book tab.

GLOBAL RECESSION - CAUSES, IMPACTS AND REMEDIES

LABOR MARKET RECOVERY AFTER THE RECESSION OF 2007-2009

SELECT ANALYSES

KYLA C. SIMS
EDITOR

NOVINKA
New York

Copyright © 2014 by Nova Science Publishers, Inc.

All rights reserved. No part of this book may be reproduced, stored in a retrieval system or transmitted in any form or by any means: electronic, electrostatic, magnetic, tape, mechanical photocopying, recording or otherwise without the written permission of the Publisher.

For permission to use material from this book please contact us:
Telephone 631-231-7269; Fax 631-231-8175
Web Site: http://www.novapublishers.com

NOTICE TO THE READER

The Publisher has taken reasonable care in the preparation of this book, but makes no expressed or implied warranty of any kind and assumes no responsibility for any errors or omissions. No liability is assumed for incidental or consequential damages in connection with or arising out of information contained in this book. The Publisher shall not be liable for any special, consequential, or exemplary damages resulting, in whole or in part, from the readers' use of, or reliance upon, this material. Any parts of this book based on government reports are so indicated and copyright is claimed for those parts to the extent applicable to compilations of such works.

Independent verification should be sought for any data, advice or recommendations contained in this book. In addition, no responsibility is assumed by the publisher for any injury and/or damage to persons or property arising from any methods, products, instructions, ideas or otherwise contained in this publication.

This publication is designed to provide accurate and authoritative information with regard to the subject matter covered herein. It is sold with the clear understanding that the Publisher is not engaged in rendering legal or any other professional services. If legal or any other expert assistance is required, the services of a competent person should be sought. FROM A DECLARATION OF PARTICIPANTS JOINTLY ADOPTED BY A COMMITTEE OF THE AMERICAN BAR ASSOCIATION AND A COMMITTEE OF PUBLISHERS.

Additional color graphics may be available in the e-book version of this book.

Library of Congress Cataloging-in-Publication Data

ISBN: 978-1-63117-890-0

Published by Nova Science Publishers, Inc. † New York

CONTENTS

PREFACE

This book discusses this slow recovery of the labor market, as well as assesses the relative magnitudes of cyclical and structural unemployment as they respond to different policy measures.

Chapter 1 – The deep recession that began in December 2007, when the economy began to contract, and ended in June 2009, when the economy began to expand again, has had a lasting effect on the labor market. More than four and a half years after the end of the recession, employment has risen sluggishly—much more slowly than it grew, on average, during the four previous recoveries that lasted more than one year. At the same time, the unemployment rate has fallen only partway back to its prerecession level, and a significant part of that improvement is attributable to a decline in labor force participation that has occurred as an unusually large number of people have stopped looking for work. To a large degree, the slow recovery of the labor market reflects the slow growth in the demand for goods and services, and hence gross domestic product (GDP). The Congressional Budget Office (CBO) estimates that GDP was 71/2 percent smaller than potential (maximum sustainable) GDP at the end of the recession; by the end of 2013, less than one-half of that gap had been closed. With output growing so slowly, payrolls have increased slowly as well—and the slack in the labor market that can be seen in the elevated unemployment rate and part of the reduction in the rate of labor force participation mirrors the gap between actual and potential GDP. To a smaller degree, the slow recovery of the labor market is the result of structural factors that stem from the recession and the slow recovery of output but that are not directly related to the economy's current cyclical weakness. For example, an exceptionally large number of people have been unemployed for long periods, and the stigma attached to their long-term unemployment, along with a possible erosion of their job skills, has made it difficult for them to find new work. In assessing the slow recovery of the labor market, CBO estimates the following: Of the roughly 2 percentage-point net increase in the rate of unemployment between the end of 2007 and the end of 2013, about 1 percentage point was the result of cyclical weakness in the demand for goods and services, and about 1 percentage point arose from structural factors; those factors are chiefly the stigma workers face and the erosion of skills that can stem from long-term unemployment (together worth about one-half of a percentage point of increase in the unemployment rate) and a decrease in the efficiency with which employers are filling vacancies (probably at least in part as a result of mismatches in skills and locations, and also worth about one-half of a percentage point of the increase in the unemployment rate). Of the roughly 3 percentage-point net decline in the labor force participation rate between the end of 2007 and the end of 2013, about 11/2 percentage points was the result of long-term trends (primarily the aging of the population), about 1 percentage point was the result of temporary weakness in employment prospects and wages, and about one-half of a percentage point was attributable to unusual aspects of the slow recovery that led workers to become discouraged and permanently drop out of the labor force. Employment at the end of 2013 was about 6 million jobs short of where it would be if the unemployment rate had returned to its prerecession level and if the participation rate had risen to the level it would have attained without the current cyclical weakness. Those factors account roughly equally for the shortfall. CBO expects that, under current laws governing federal taxes and spending, output will grow more rapidly in the next few years than it has in the recent past but recovery in the labor market will continue for some time.[1] The agency projects that by the second half of 2017, the gap between actual and potential GDP will return to its average historical relationship—bringing the effects of cyclical conditions on unemployment and labor force participation back to their average values in 2018. However, CBO projects, the aging of the population will further reduce labor force participation during the coming decade, and the longer-lasting effects of the recession and slow recovery on unemployment and the size of the labor force will continue, albeit with diminishing magnitude, throughout the decade. All told, CBO projects that the unemployment rate will fall to 5.8 percent by the end of 2017 and to 5.5 percent by 2024 (compared with 4.8 percent at the end of 2007) and that the labor force participation rate will decline to 60.8 percent by 2024 (compared with 66.0 percent at the end of 2007).

Chapter 2 – The unemployment rate greatly increased after the onset of the latest recession in December 2007, when it measured 5.0%. The rate peaked at 10.0% in October 2009, four months after the recession's official end in June 2009. More than three years into the recovery, the unemployment rate averaged 8.1% in 2012. Given its still elevated level, policymakers may continue to be concerned about how to spur economic growth and create jobs. Over the past few years, Congress has used fiscal policy and the Federal Reserve (Fed) has used monetary policy to put the economy on a path toward the level of demand for goods and services that preceded the 2007-2009 recession. Firms react to recessions by laying off workers, and the deeper the downturn in the business cycle, the greater the rise in unemployment that results. Expansionary fiscal and monetary policies commonly have been used to remedy what is known as cyclical unemployment. The unemployment rate has not been as responsive as had been hoped to the countercyclical measures undertaken by Congress and the Fed. Consequently, some have suggested that an increase in another type of unemployment—referred to as structural unemployment—has accounted for much of the rise in the unemployment rate from pre-recession levels. These observers assert that the rise in unemployment due to change in the structure of the economy represents "a new normal" of elevated unemployment rates for years to come. Structural unemployment develops for different reasons than cyclical unemployment. Structural unemployment results when jobseekers do not move quickly into vacant jobs. Obstacles that lengthen the spell of unemployment (i.e., prolong the period of job search) include mismatches between the skills or locations of jobless workers and the skill requirements or locations of available jobs. Another impediment is the composition of the unemployed, such as more workers whose connection to their former employers is permanently severed (i.e., fewer workers likely to be recalled from layoffs once business revives at their former employers). A third factor that may contribute to long-term unemployment is known as labor market institutions, such as unemployment benefit programs. The measures enacted by Congress have chiefly focused on alleviating cyclical unemployment. To the extent that the still-high unemployment rate results from the slow pace of output growth during the recovery, economic theory suggests that fiscal and monetary stimulus would be suitable strategies for further reducing joblessness. To the extent that structural factors have contributed to the still-high unemployment rate, economic theory suggests measures such as promoting the education and retraining of workers who permanently lost jobs in hard-hit industries (e.g., home building) so that they can acquire the skills needed to obtain employment in other industries. This report assesses the relative magnitudes of cyclical and structural unemployment as they respond to different policy measures. An analysis of changes since 2007 in a variety of labor market indicators across industries and areas finds patterns that strongly suggest most of the increase in the U.S. unemployment rate is cyclical (i.e., due to depressed aggregate demand). Empirical studies suggest that, although structural unemployment has temporarily increased, it accounted for a minority of the rise in the unemployment rate in recent years.

Chapter 3 – A persistently high unemployment rate is of concern to Congress for a variety of reasons, including its negative consequences for the economic well-being of individuals and its impact on the federal budget. The unemployment rate was 9.5% when the economy emerged from the 11th postwar recession in June 2009. It climbed further to peak at 10.0% in October 2009. The rate has slowly declined since then. Although it dropped below 8% in the fourth quarter of 2012, the unemployment rate remains high by historical standards. After most postwar recessions, it took at least eight months for the unemployment rate to fall by one full percentage point. The slowest decline occurred following the 2001 recession's end, when the unemployment rate was a comparatively low 5.5%. About 31/2 years elapsed before the rate fell just one-half of one percentage point. In contrast, the recovery from the severe 1981-1982 recession began with the highest unemployment rate of the postwar period (10.8%). In that instance, it took only eight months for the rate to fall over one percentage point. Some hoped the unemployment rate would fall as quickly after the 2007-2009 recession, but the speed of improvement has been more typical of the so-called jobless recoveries from the 2001 and 1990- 1991 recessions. What appears to matter for a reduction in the unemployment rate is the size of the output gap, that is, the rate of actual output (economic) growth compared with the rate of potential output growth. Potential output is a measure of the economy's capacity to produce goods and services when resources (e.g., labor) are fully utilized. The growth rate of potential output is a function of the growth rates of potential productivity and the labor supply when the economy is at full employment. If potential output growth is about 2.5% annually at full employment, then the growth rate in real gross domestic product (GDP) would have to be greater to yield a falling unemployment rate. How much greater will determine the speed of improvement in the unemployment rate, according to a rule of thumb known as Okun's law. In its August 2012 economic forecast, the Congressional Budget Office (CBO) estimates that the annual average growth rate of real GDP will gradually approach the growth rate of potential output over the 2012-2022 projection period. As a result of this slow narrowing of the output gap, the unemployment rate is forecast to 5.9% by 2017.

Chapter 4 – New information that adds to the mix of labor market indicators may be useful to Congress. The ratio of unemployed persons per job opening provides information on how many unemployed persons on average there are for every job opening. It adds to the current mix of labor market indicators such as the unemployment rate, which is a measure of the excess supply of workers. In addition, it adds to employment statistics, which measures the demand for workers that have already been met by employers. By dividing the number of unemployed persons with the number of job openings, the ratio gauges the excess supply of workers relative to the demand, where job openings serve as a measure of the unmet need for workers. The resultant statistic compares the number of persons who are actively searching for jobs to the number of available opportunities. Four key findings arise from this analysis: The ratio of unemployed persons per job opening is highly correlated with the unemployment rate between 2001 and 2012. The ratio of unemployed persons per job opening rises during the recessionary periods covered in this data set. In the 2007-2009 recession, the ratio rises to very high levels, especially in the goods-producing industries (construction, manufacturing, mining and logging). Although the ratio is highly correlated with changes in the unemployment rate, the ratio saw modest improvements coming out of the recent recession sooner than the reductions in the unemployment rate. Even though the ratio has reduced, it remains at higher levels than prior to the 2007-2009 recession. The analysis in this report combines two data sources: The *Job Openings and Labor Turnover Survey (JOLTS)*, which provide information from a survey of U.S. business establishments on the dynamic job market where job openings are created, persons are hired, and employees leave. The *Current Population Survey (CPS)*, which provides information on economic and demographic information from U.S. households.

In: Labor Market Recovery …
Editor: Kyla C. Sims
ISBN: 978-1-63117-890-0
© 2014 Nova Science Publishers, Inc.

Chapter 1

THE SLOW RECOVERY OF THE LABOR MARKET*

David Brauer and Charles Whalen

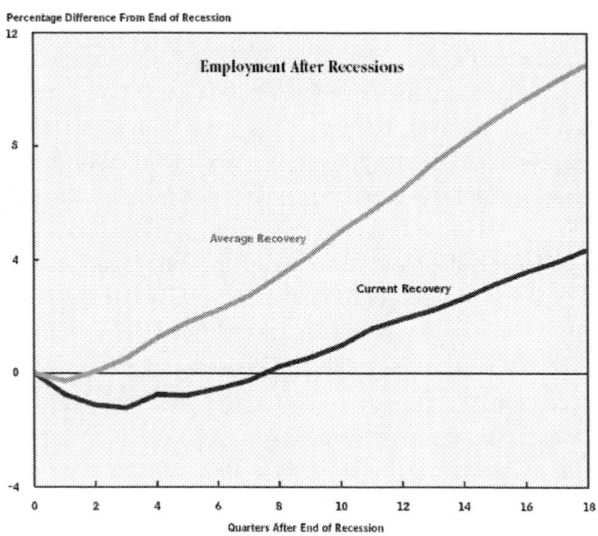

This chart shows postrecession employment of all workers on nonfarm payrolls; it does not include data revisions released by the Bureau of Labor

* This is an edited, reformatted and augmented version of a report released by the Congressional Budget Office, dated February 2014.

Statistics in February 2014. The line showing the average recovery is derived from data for the periods after the recessions ending in March 1975, November 1982, March 1991, and November 2001.

NOTES

Numbers in the text may not add up to totals because of rounding.

The figures show vertical bars to indicate the duration of recessions. (A recession extends from the peak of a business cycle to its trough.)

SUMMARY

The deep recession that began in December 2007, when the economy began to contract, and ended in June 2009, when the economy began to expand again, has had a lasting effect on the labor market. More than four and a half years after the end of the recession, employment has risen sluggishly—much more slowly than it grew, on average, during the four previous recoveries that lasted more than one year. At the same time, the unemployment rate has fallen only partway back to its prerecession level, and a significant part of that improvement is attributable to a decline in labor force participation that has occurred as an unusually large number of people have stopped looking for work.

To a large degree, the slow recovery of the labor market reflects the slow growth in the demand for goods and services, and hence gross domestic product (GDP). The Congressional Budget Office (CBO) estimates that GDP was 71/2 percent smaller than potential (maximum sustainable) GDP at the end of the recession; by the end of 2013, less than one-half of that gap had been closed. With output growing so slowly, payrolls have increased slowly as well—and the slack in the labor market that can be seen in the elevated unemployment rate and part of the reduction in the rate of labor force participation mirrors the gap between actual and potential GDP.

To a smaller degree, the slow recovery of the labor market is the result of structural factors that stem from the recession and the slow recovery of output but that are not directly related to the economy's current cyclical weakness. For example, an exceptionally large number of people have been unemployed for long periods, and the stigma attached to their long-term unemployment, along with a possible erosion of their job skills, has made it difficult for them to find new work.

In assessing the slow recovery of the labor market, CBO estimates the following:

- Of the roughly 2 percentage-point net increase in the rate of unemployment between the end of 2007 and the end of 2013, about 1 percentage point was the result of cyclical weakness in the demand for goods and services, and about 1 percentage point arose from structural factors; those factors are chiefly the stigma workers face and the erosion of skills that can stem from long-term unemployment (together worth about one-half of a percentage point of increase in the unemployment rate) and a decrease in the efficiency with which employers are filling vacancies (probably at least in part as a result of mismatches in skills and locations, and also worth about one-half of a percentage point of the increase in the unemployment rate).
- Of the roughly 3 percentage-point net decline in the labor force participation rate between the end of 2007 and the end of 2013, about 11/2 percentage points was the result of long-term trends (primarily the aging of the population), about 1 percentage point was the result of temporary weakness in employment prospects and wages, and about one-half of a percentage point was attributable to unusual aspects of the slow recovery that led workers to become discouraged and permanently drop out of the labor force.
- Employment at the end of 2013 was about 6 million jobs short of where it would be if the unemployment rate had returned to its prerecession level and if the participation rate had risen to the level it would have attained without the current cyclical weakness. Those factors account roughly equally for the shortfall.

CBO expects that, under current laws governing federal taxes and spending, output will grow more rapidly in the next few years than it has in the recent past but recovery in the labor market will continue for some time.[1] The agency projects that by the second half of 2017, the gap between actual and potential GDP will return to its average historical relationship—bringing the effects of cyclical conditions on unemployment and labor force participation back to their average values in 2018. However, CBO projects, the aging of the population will further reduce labor force participation during the coming decade, and the longer-lasting effects of the recession and slow recovery on unemployment and the size of the labor force will continue, albeit with diminishing magnitude, throughout the decade. All told, CBO projects that the unemployment rate will fall to 5.8 percent by the end of 2017 and to 5.5 percent by 2024 (compared with 4.8 percent at the end of 2007) and that the labor force participation rate will decline to 60.8 percent by 2024 (compared with 66.0 percent at the end of 2007).

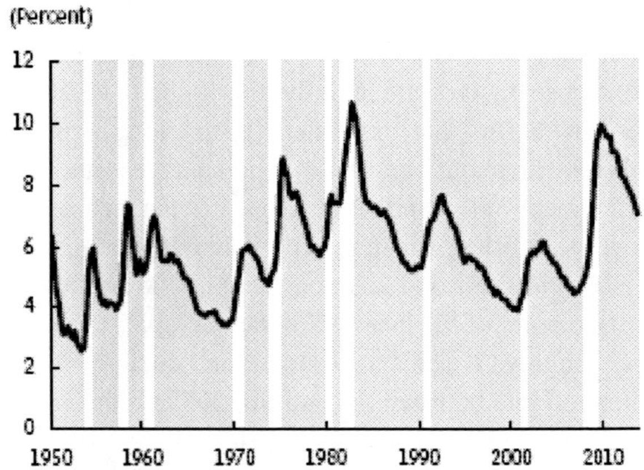

Sources: Congressional Budget Office; Bureau of Labor Statistics.

Notes: The unemployment rate is a measure of the number of jobless people who are available for and actively seeking work, expressed as a percentage of the labor force. Data are quarterly and are plotted through 2013.

Figure 1. Unemployment Rate.

The pace and nature of the economic recovery have been difficult to predict, and the path of the economy and the labor market will no doubt hold surprises as well. CBO's projections of the labor market are subject to several sources of uncertainty, and many developments could cause outcomes substantially different from those CBO has projected.

DEVELOPMENTS IN THE LABOR MARKET SINCE THE RECESSION

The U.S. labor market has recovered slowly and only partially since June 2009, when the recession ended. Evidence of a weak recovery appears in the data on employment, unemployment, labor force participation, and other indicators of labor market activity. Although the recession ended more than four and a half years ago, the unemployment rate and, notably, the rate of longterm unemployment are still high; the labor force participation rate is well below its trend; and employment has not returned to its prerecession peak.

Unemployment Rates

The share of people in the labor force who are unemployed has fallen in recent years but remains high (see Figure 1).[2] It fell to 7.0 percent in the fourth quarter of 2013 (and 6.7 percent in December) after having reached a peak of almost 10 percent in the fourth quarter of 2009. Although the unemployment rate has reversed more than half its rise during the recession, it remains high by historical standards; its slow decline since the recent peak reflects in part the slowest recovery in employment following a recession since 1975 (except for the recession during 1980, which was followed by another recession only 12 months later).

Although the rate of long-term unemployment—the percentage of the labor force that has been out of work for more than 26 consecutive weeks—also has declined in the past few years, it remains extraordinarily high (see Figure 2).

The long-term unemployment rate was 0.8 percent in 2007; by the second quarter of 2010 it had surged to 4.3 percent. Although that rate has since declined to 2.6 percent, it is still higher than at any time between 1948 (when such data were first collected) and 2008. The long-term unemployed currently number about 4 million, compared with 1.3 million before the recession. In contrast, the share of the labor force that has been unemployed for less than five weeks rose from 1.7 percent to 2.1 percent during the recession and by 2011 had fallen back to close to its prerecession level; the share of the labor force that has been unemployed for 5 to 26 weeks rose from 2.2 percent to 4.7 percent during the recession but fell to 2.8 percent at the end of 2013.

Broader indicators in the labor market also have improved only slowly. For example, the Bureau of Labor Statistics publishes a measure of underutilization in the labor market called U-6, which combines the number of unemployed people with numbers for two other groups of people: those who are "marginally attached" to the labor force (that is, who are not currently looking for work but are willing and able to work and who have looked for work in the past 12 months) and part-time employees who work less than 35 hours per week in all jobs for economic reasons (either because of slack work or business conditions or because they cannot find full-time employment).

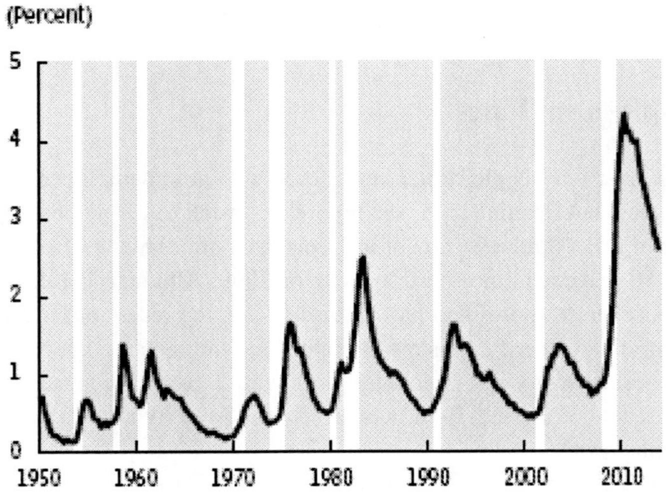

Sources: Congressional Budget Office; Bureau of Labor Statistics.

Notes: The rate of long-term unemployment is the percentage of the labor force that has been out of work for more than 26 consecutive weeks. Data are quarterly and are plotted through 2013. The data before 1994 are not strictly comparable with the later data.

Figure 2. Rate of Long-Term Unemployment.

By the fourth quarter of 2013, declines in the number of people in each of those groups had reduced the U-6 measure to 13.3 percent, a notable improvement relative to the 17.1 percent mark in the fourth quarter of 2009 but still significantly above the 8.5 percent reading in the fourth quarter of 2007 (see Figure 3).

The share of employees who usually work part time rose during the recession, reaching 20 percent in 2010, compared with 17 percent in 2007. Although most people who work part time do so for noneconomic reasons, those who worked part time for economic reasons accounted for more than the entire increase in the share of employees working part time. That share has declined slowly but steadily since the end of the recession (although it remains above prerecession levels), and people who work part time for economic reasons have accounted for more than the entire decline (see Figure 4).

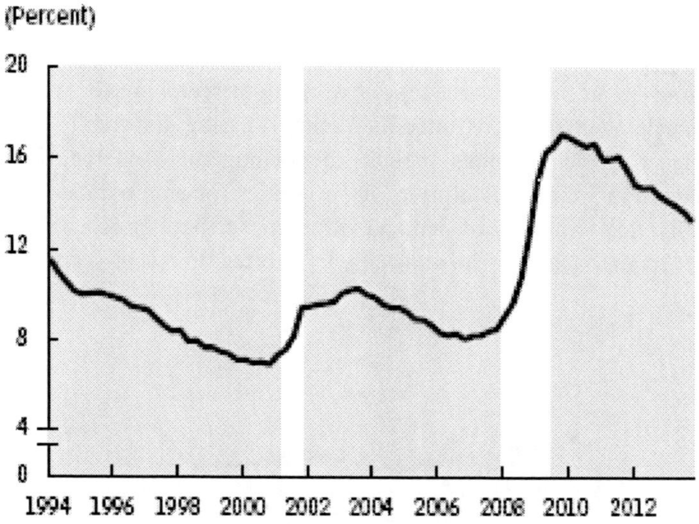

Sources: Congressional Budget Office; Bureau of Labor Statistics.

Notes: This measure of the underutilization of labor, called U-6, combines the total number of people who are unemployed, those who are marginally attached to the labor force (who are not currently looking for work but are willing and able to work and have looked for work in the past 12 months), and those who work part time for economic reasons. It is expressed as a percentage of the labor force plus the number of marginally attached workers. Data are quarterly and are plotted through 2013.

Figure 3. Underutilization of Labor.

Patterns of unemployment by age, sex, and educational attainment indicate that no group has been spared in the weak labor market. However, the increase in unemployment during the recession was most pronounced among men and among some categories of workers with higherthan-average unemployment rates before the recession (such as people under age 25 and those without a high school diploma). Unemployment rates for all major categories of workers have declined over the past several years, reversing between half and three-fourths of their earlier increases, but they are still high.

Labor Force Participation

Another striking consequence of the weak labor market has been the sharp decline in the labor force participation rate, the percentage of people in the civilian noninstitutionalized population who are age 16 or older and either working or actively seeking work (see Figure 5). That rate reflects people's decisions about the attractiveness of working or searching for work compared with such alternatives as attending school, caring for family members, or retiring. Key determinants include the demographic characteristics of the population and the availability of opportunities for employment. Participation typically falls when labor demand is weak, but poor prospects in the labor market seem to have had an unusually large effect in recent years.

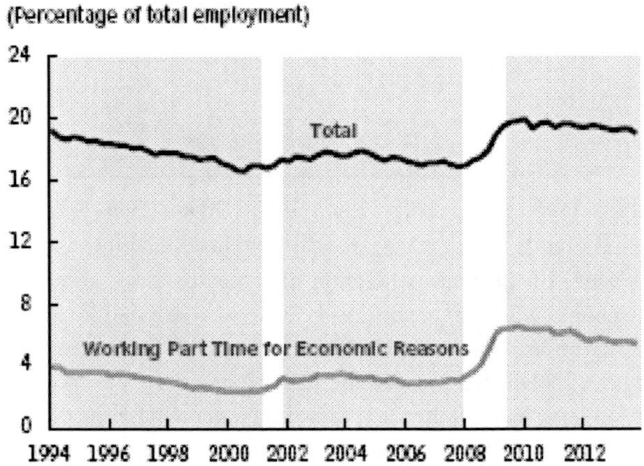

Sources: Congressional Budget Office; Bureau of Labor Statistics.

Notes: Part-time employees are people who usually work less than 35 hours per week. The share of part-time employment for economic reasons is the percentage of workers who work part time because of slack work or business conditions or because they cannot find full-time employment. Data are quarterly and are plotted through 2013.

Figure 4. Share of Workers Who Are Employed Part Time.

The labor force participation rate edged downward by about one-quarter of a percentage point during the 2007–2009 recession, and it has fallen by about 23/4 percentage points since the end of the recession—to 62.9 percent in the fourth quarter of 2013, the lowest rate since 1978. The postrecession decline partly reflects the aging of the baby-boom generation, whose members have been reaching typical retirement ages (the oldest of the group turned 65 in 2011). But it also reflects declining participation within some age groups. For men between the ages of 25 and 54, participation, which had been falling gradually over a period of four decades, fell by another 1.4 percentage points from 2009 to 2013. Participation among women in the same age group rose steadily between the 1950s and late 1990s, but then flattened for several years and fell by 1.8 percentage points from 2009 to 2013. Participation among men and women under age 25 fell by 1.8 percentage points between 2009 and 2013, a decline that was roughly in line with its trend over the previous decade. And participation among people between the ages of 55 and 64, which had been rising before the recession, has edged slightly lower since 2009. In contrast, the pronounced upward trend in the participation rate among people age 65 or older since the mid-1990s has continued.

Employment

Employment has picked up since the recession, but it has grown slowly, and employers now report having about 1 million fewer workers on their payrolls than they had in early 2008. The number of employees in nonfarm jobs peaked at 138 million in the first quarter of 2008 and fell to 129 million by the first quarter of 2010; since then, nonfarm employment has been on an upward trend, although it is still not quite 137 million—notwithstanding the growth in the U.S. population since 2008 (see Figure 6).[3]

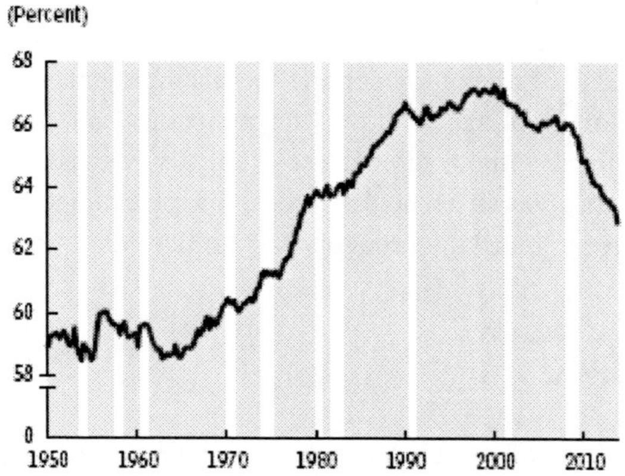

Sources: Congressional Budget Office; Bureau of Labor Statistics.

Notes: The rate of participation in the labor force is the percentage of the civilian noninstitutionalized population age 16 or older that is either working or available for and actively seeking work. Data are quarterly and are plotted through 2013.

Figure 5. Rate of Participation in the Labor Force.

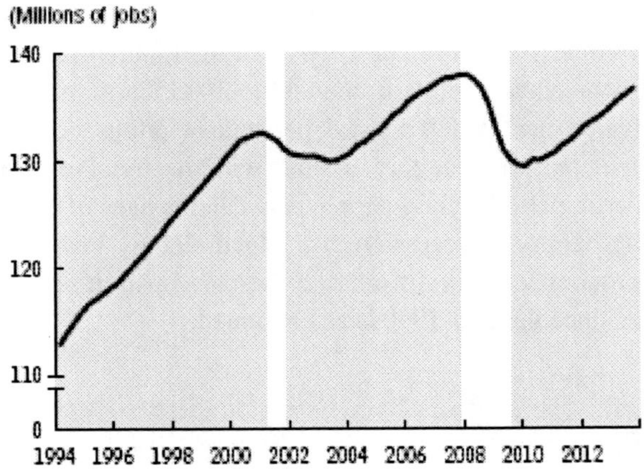

Sources: Congressional Budget Office; Bureau of Labor Statistics.

Notes: Nonfarm employment consists of all employees on nonfarm payrolls. Data are quarterly and are plotted through 2013.

Figure 6. Total Nonfarm Employment.

In fact, employment has recovered essentially none of its dramatic decline as a share of the population. The employment-to-population ratio fell sharply from its prerecession peak of 63.3 percent in the fourth quarter of 2006 and now is barely above its postrecession low of 58.3 percent (see Figure 7).[4] That change reflects both the decline in the rate of labor force participation and the increase in the rate of unemployment. If the unemployment rate had returned to its prerecession level and if the participation rate had risen to the level it would have attained without the current cyclical weakness, the employment-to-population ratio would be 60.8 percent, 2.3 percentage points above the current 58.5 percent, translating roughly to 6 million jobs.

Other Indicators

Other indicators of conditions in the labor market suggest that although fewer people are becoming unemployed, finding work is still unusually difficult. After rising during the recession, layoffs and discharges from employment have fallen back below their prerecession rates. As a result, initial claims for unemployment insurance (UI) benefits, which more than doubled during the recession, also are close to prerecession rates (based on a four-week moving average, which reduces the weekto-week volatility in this measure). In addition, the incidence of people quitting their jobs has increased, perhaps reflecting workers' improved perceptions about their ability to find new employment. Hiring, however, remains well below its prerecession rate, and, as a consequence, the probability that an unemployed person will find a job within a given period is significantly less than it was before the recession. Indeed, the number of job seekers for each open job is still high: That ratio was 1.8 in December 2007, it reached a peak of 6.7 in July 2009, and then dropped to 2.7 by November 2013.

The slow recovery of the labor market has depressed growth in labor compensation (the combination of wages, salaries, and benefits that workers receive). Hourly wages and compensation for private industry workers grew at an annual rate of about 3 percent in the years just before the recession; but since then, they have grown at a rate of about 2 percent annually (see Figure 8).[5]

In real (inflation-adjusted) terms, hourly compensation in the third quarter of 2013 was only 0.5 percent above its mark in the second quarter of 2009, at the end of the recession.

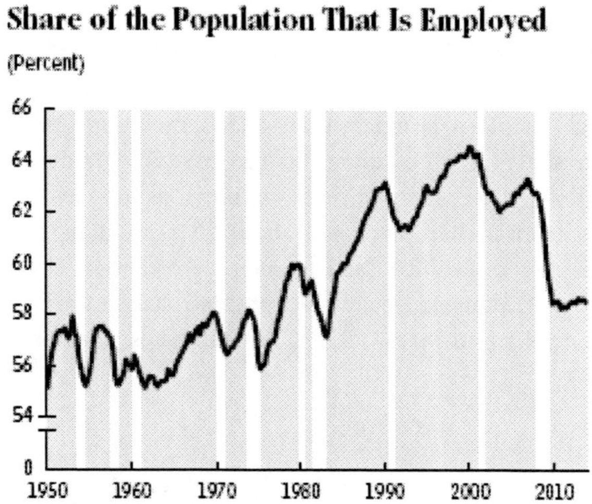

Sources: Congressional Budget Office; Bureau of Labor Statistics.

Notes: Data show the number of employed workers (as measured by the Current Population Survey) as a percentage of the civilian noninstitutionalized population age 16 or older. Data are quarterly and are plotted through 2013.

Figure 7. Share of the Population That Is Employed.

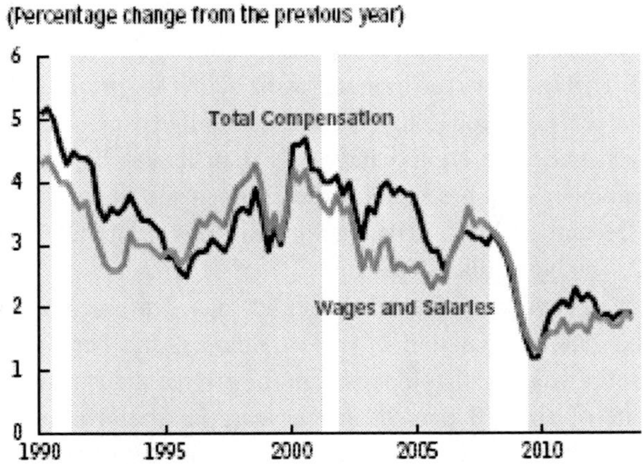

Sources: Congressional Budget Office; Bureau of Labor Statistics.

Notes: The data are employment cost indexes for workers in private industry. Total compensation is wages and salaries plus benefits. Data are quarterly and are plotted through the third quarter of 2013.

Figure 8. Hourly Labor Compensation.

The slow growth of hourly compensation, combined with the slow growth of employment, has led to a decline in the labor share of total income. Labor income, which includes compensation and some proprietors' income, has declined as a share of gross domestic income (GDI) since the end of the recession, falling more sharply than its previous downward trend.[6] CBO estimates that labor's share averaged about 57 percent in 2013, down from more than 59 percent in 2008 (and an average of about 591/2 percent since 1980). In contrast, domestic economic profits' share of GDI rose over that period, reaching 9.5 percent of GDI, CBO estimates, up from 6.8 percent in mid-2009.[7]

Interpreting Developments in the Labor Market

The improvement of the labor market during the past several years has been slow because of cyclical and structural factors. Cyclical weakness in the overall demand for goods and services, which has been the more important of the two, has hampered the growth of employment, impeded the reduction in the unemployment rate, and depressed the labor force participation rate. However, structural factors—noncyclical forces that alter the willingness and ability of unemployed workers to find jobs and of employers to find suitable workers—also have restrained the recovery in the labor market.

Causes of High Unemployment

The slow growth of the economy has been the most important determinant of the path of the unemployment rate in the years since the onset of the recession, but structural factors have played a notable role as well— and one that has become relatively more significant as the economy has improved. By the end of 2013, the causes of the roughly 2 percentage-point net increase in the rate of unemployment since the end of 2007 were identified as having been almost equally cyclical and structural, in CBO's assessment.[8] (As discussed below, the current cyclical weakness of the economy would have a larger effect on the unemployment rate if it was not also holding down the participation rate.) If the unemployment rate was back down to its prerecession level of roughly 5 percent—about 2 percentage points below the average unemployment rate in the fourth quarter of last year— about 3 million people who are currently looking for work would be employed.

Cyclical Economic Weakness

According to CBO's assessment, the slow recovery of the labor market primarily reflects the slow recovery in production, which in turn is a reflection of the slow recovery in the demand for goods and services. By the second quarter of 2009, CBO estimates, real GDP was about 71/2 percent below its potential level. From that point through the end of 2013, real output grew at an average annual rate of almost 21/2 percent, leaving it roughly 4 percent below potential GDP by the end of last year.[9] The unemployment rate typically increases when actual economic output falls short of potential output, decreasing employers' demand for workers. On average, and all else being equal, an output gap of -2 percent (when output is 2 percent below its estimated potential) has been associated with an unemployment rate that is 1 percentage point above the natural rate (the rate arising from all sources other than fluctuations in the overall demand for goods and services). In the absence of the unusual factors affecting the labor market, the application of that historical relationship to the gap between actual and estimated potential GDP at the end of 2013 suggests that the cyclical weakness of the economy was responsible for elevating the unemployment rate by about 2 percentage points.

However, the historical relationship between the output gap and the unemployment rate does not account adequately for some of the structural factors that are currently pushing up unemployment or for the unusually large decline in the labor force participation rate that is currently holding down unemployment. After accounting for those developments (as described below), CBO estimates that cyclical economic weakness is currently keeping the unemployment rate roughly 1 percentage point above what it would otherwise be.

Structural Factors

Structural factors raise both the actual rate of unemployment and the natural rate of unemployment. CBO estimates that structural factors accounted for roughly 1 percentage point of the difference between the unemployment rate at the end of 2007 and at the end of 2013. CBO also estimates that the natural rate of unemployment was 5 percent at the end of 2007 and, reflecting those structural factors, was 6 percent at the end of 2013.[10] Three structural factors, according to CBO's analysis, account for that 1 percentage-point increase:[11]

- About one-half of a percentage point is attributable to the stigma of long-term unemployment (which may cause employers to be less inclined to hire someone who has been out of work for a considerable period, out of concern that the person might be a less desirable worker) and the erosion of workers' skills that can attend long-term unemployment.
- About one-half of a percentage point is attributable to a decrease in the efficiency with which employers filled vacancies, probably at least in part as a result of mismatches between the needs of employers and the skills and locations of those seeking work.
- About one-tenth of a percentage point is attributable to the incentives generated in 2013 by extensions of UI benefits (from the usual 26 weeks to as much as 99 weeks), primarily because the program's rules led some people to remain in the labor force and to continue to search for work in order to remain eligible. (The effect of that factor on the unemployment rate was greater in earlier years during and after the recession when more people were receiving extended benefits.)

Evidence that factors other than weakness in overall demand for goods and services are boosting the unemployment rate comes in part from a shift in what is known as the Beveridge curve—the relationship between the job vacancy rate (the ratio of openings to total employment) and the unemployment rate (see Figure 9). That shift, an increase in the unemployment rate for any given job vacancy rate, suggests either that unemployed workers are facing unusual difficulties finding suitable work in the available jobs (as would result from the difficulties faced by the long-term unemployed or from a decrease in the efficiency with which employers and job seekers are matched) or that the labor force is growing for reasons that are unrelated to the strength in the economy (as would result from extensions of UI benefits).[12]

Stigma and the Erosion of Skills. Long-term unemployment can lead to subsequent difficulties in securing work. The stigma of being out of work for an extended period tends to worsen employment prospects. Another barrier is created by the erosion of skills that can come from long-term unemployment. Although the extent to which those factors increased unemployment during and after the recession is difficult to quantify, the probability of finding a job is significantly lower for the long-term unemployed than it is for people who have spent less time out of work.

Sources: Congressional Budget Office; Bureau of Labor Statistics.

Notes: The job vacancy rate is the number of job openings, expressed as a percentage of the sum of total nonfarm employment plus job openings. The unemployment rate is a measure of the number of jobless people who are available for and actively seeking work, expressed as a percentage of the labor force. Data are monthly and are plotted from January 2001 through November 2013.

Figure 9. Beveridge Curve: Relationship Between Job Vacancies and Unemployment.

On the basis of that finding and other findings in research, CBO estimates that the stigma and erosion of skills arising from the unusually large number of the long-term unemployed accounted for about one-half of a percentage point of the net increase in the unemployment rate from the beginning of the recession to the end of last year.[13] That effect has grown over time, and CBO expects it to persist for several years before gradually abating, as some of the long-term unemployed either retire or leave the labor force in some other way and as others eventually obtain stable jobs.

Matching Unemployed Workers with Available Jobs

In well-functioning labor markets, job seekers and employers efficiently find mutually beneficial matches. Individual businesses grow and shrink in response to fluctuations in profitability and in the demand for their products; workers change jobs as they look for and find positions that best fit their skills and interests; and improvements in technology, changing consumer preferences, and changes in international trade have disproportionate effects on various industries, occupations, and locations of work. The need for workers to move from one industry or occupation to another, to acquire new skills to facilitate such a shift, or to relocate to find new work often is characterized as a skill or locational mismatch, and such mismatches always result in some amount of unemployment as businesses with vacancies and workers looking for jobs take time to find good matches. That normal mismatch is one component of CBO's estimate of the natural rate of unemployment, which was 5 percent before the recession.

Mismatches can become more important when unusual advances in technology or shifts in the demand for various products require significant changes in the distribution of workers among industries, occupations, or locations. For example, because the demand for construction workers declined sharply during the recession as a result of the collapse of the housing market, many affected workers sought employment in other occupations. Separately, some of the increase in the difficulty of matching unemployed workers with available jobs appears to have occurred because employers are recruiting less intensively than they have in the past to fill vacant jobs, independent of any changes in the suitability of the pool of candidates.[14]

CBO estimates that increased difficulties matching workers with jobs accounted for about one-half of a percentage point of the net increase in the unemployment rate from the beginning of the recession to the end of 2013. That effect will diminish gradually over the next few years, in CBO's judgment, as the causes of dampened matching efficiency recede and as workers acquire new skills, shift to faster growing industries and occupations, or relocate to take advantage of new opportunities.

Extensions of UI Benefits

In response to the high unemployment caused by the recession, legislation to provide emergency unemployment compensation (EUC) was enacted that allowed states to provide additional weeks of federally funded unemployment benefits to people who had exhausted their regular state benefits.[15] In CBO's judgment, those expansions had several effects on unemployment and on employment.

First, the availability of EUC discouraged some recipients from taking jobs they considered unsuitable because the additional benefits reduced the hardship of being unemployed, and the legislation required recipients to continue to search for employment and to remain in the labor force in order to continue to receive benefits. Although those incentives increased unemployment among recipients, the weight of the evidence suggests that their effect was small.[16]

Second, the availability of EUC affected the employment of prospective workers who were ineligible for benefits, such as new entrants and reentrants to the labor force. To the extent that beneficiaries were less likely to accept available jobs, those who were unemployed but not receiving benefits were more likely to obtain and accept job offers. Given the elevated unemployment rate, nearly all of the jobs that were not taken by people receiving EUC were instead taken by others who were searching for work, in CBO's view.

CBO estimates that those effects on incentives, taken together, had little effect on employment but, by boosting the number of people in the labor force, they increased the rate of unemployment by as much as one-third of a percentage point during the past several years. However, the size of the effects diminished in 2013, as the number of people exhausting their regular state benefits declined and as new legislation trimmed the availability of EUC; by the fourth quarter of 2013, those effects boosted the unemployment rate by one-tenth of a percentage point, CBO estimates.

Separately, by putting money in the hands of people who spent much of it on goods and services, UI benefits increased the demand for workers to produce those goods and services, indirectly raising total employment compared with what it would have been otherwise. Taking into account the effects both on incentives and on spending, CBO estimates that in late 2013 the benefits provided by the EUC program raised employment by about 200,000.[17] Combining that effect on employment with the increase in the labor force resulting from recipients' continuing to look for work in order to receive benefits, CBO estimates that the extension of UI benefits had little net effect on the unemployment rate at the end of 2013.

Causes of Low Labor Force Participation

According to CBO's analysis, the unusually low rate of labor force participation in recent years is attributable to three principal factors: long-term trends, especially the aging of the population; temporary weakness in employment prospects and wages; and some longer-term factors attributable to the unusual aspects of the slow recovery of the labor market, including persistently low hiring rates. Of the 3 percentage-point decline in participation between the end of 2007 and the end of 2013, CBO estimates, about 11/2 percentage points was the result of long-term trends, about 1 percentage point arose from temporary weakness in employment prospects and wages, and about one-half of a percentage point was attributable to unusual aspects of the slow recovery.

Long-Term Trends

During the past six years, the participation rate has declined by roughly 11/2 percentage points because of long-term trends, CBO estimates. That decline is attributable mostly to retirement of members of the baby-boom generation. The aging of that generation has increased the share of people who are age 55 or older and are thus less likely to work than younger people. In addition, underlying trends in the participation rate within groups of people of a given age or by sex have contributed slightly to the decline in the overall participation rate since 2007. For example, those trends suggest declining participation for people under 25 and roughly stable labor force participation rate for women in their prime working years (ages 25 to 54), which had risen rapidly from the 1960s to the 1980s. (CBO expects that, in coming years, the aging of the population will continue to push down the overall participation rate but underlying trends in the participation rate within groups will have little net effect on the overall participation rate.)[18]

Temporary Factors

During periods of cyclical economic weakness, a lack of good job opportunities discourages some people from searching for employment and encourages some people to stay in school instead of seeking work. As a result, the labor force participation rate tends to decline during economic downturns and rebound during recoveries.

The recent weakness in the economy has led to what CBO judges to be a temporary drop of roughly 1 percentage point in the participation rate since 2007. That decline corresponds to roughly 3 million people who have left the labor force or are staying out of it until more jobs are available. Continued recovery of the economy will increase the demand for workers, drawing those people back into the labor force. Thus, CBO projects that the dampening effect on labor force participation will have dwindled by 2018, a year after actual GDP is projected to return to its historical relationship with potential GDP.

A slight offset to that reduction in labor force participation comes from two other aspects of the recession and slow recovery. First, at the depths of the recession, when sharply falling prices for housing and equities caused a precipitous decline in wealth, a significant number of older people appear to have postponed retirement or otherwise stayed in the labor force to preserve or restore their financial well-being.[19] Second, CBO estimates that the extension of UI benefits modestly boosted labor force participation (as discussed earlier).

Longer-Term Factors Attributable to Unusual Aspects of the Slow Recovery

The limited opportunities for unemployed job seekers in recent years will also have long-term effects on people's participation in the labor force, especially on the participation of people who have been unemployed for a long time. The unusually protracted weakness in the demand for labor appears to have led some workers to become discouraged and permanently drop out of the labor force, a longer-term factor that CBO estimates accounts for about one-half of a percentage point of the decrease in the participation rate since 2007.

In part, the permanent withdrawal from the labor force among those unemployed workers is evident in a rise in the number of people applying for and receiving benefits from the Social Security Disability Insurance program, which provides benefits to nonelderly adults who have held jobs but who are judged to be unable to perform "substantial" work because of a disability.[20] In CBO's view, the difficulty of finding work during the past several years made it worthwhile for some unemployed people with moderate disabilities to apply for benefits rather than search for employment that would accommodate their disabilities. Indeed, the number of applications to the program averaged 2.8 million per year between 2009 and 2013, up from an annual average of 2.2

million during the previous five years. Once enrolled, very few recipients leave the program to return to the labor force.

Other people also have left the labor force and will not return—in CBO's view, because of the recession and slow recovery—without applying for disability benefits. For example, the weakness in the labor market has led some older workers to retire earlier than they otherwise would have and to remain out of the labor force permanently. In addition, some unemployed workers who were unable to find suitable new jobs chose alternative unpaid activities, such as caring for family members, and will remain out of the labor force permanently.

The effect of long-term factors on the participation rate that has stemmed from the recession and its aftermath— inducing people to leave the labor force permanently—is expected to diminish slowly. Over time, those who have left for that reason will reach retirement age or otherwise come to a point at which they would have left the labor force regardless of the strength of the labor market. As the effects of the recession and its aftermath wane, future changes in labor force participation will be determined by long-run trends in demographics.

CBO's Labor Market Projections for the Next Decade

CBO expects that, under current laws governing federal taxes and spending, the labor market will strengthen considerably during the coming years because of a continued economic expansion and a lessening of the structural factors that have weighed on employment. CBO projects that the unemployment rate will fall to 5.8 percent by the end of 2017 and to 5.5 percent by 2024, reflecting declines in both cyclical and structural unemployment. CBO also projects that the downward pressure on the labor force participation rate from the recession and slow recovery will abate but that demographic trends and federal fiscal policies will diminish labor force participation—leading to a further decline in that rate during the next decade.

Nevertheless, a strengthening economy and the growth of the population will cause payroll employment in the nonfarm business sector to increase from about 137 million at the end of 2013 to about 149 million at the end of 2024, CBO projects.

In addition, CBO anticipates that growth in real hourly labor compensation will pick up as the demand for workers increases. The agency also expects that the share of total income earned by labor will increase over the decade but will not reach its average level of the past few decades.[21]

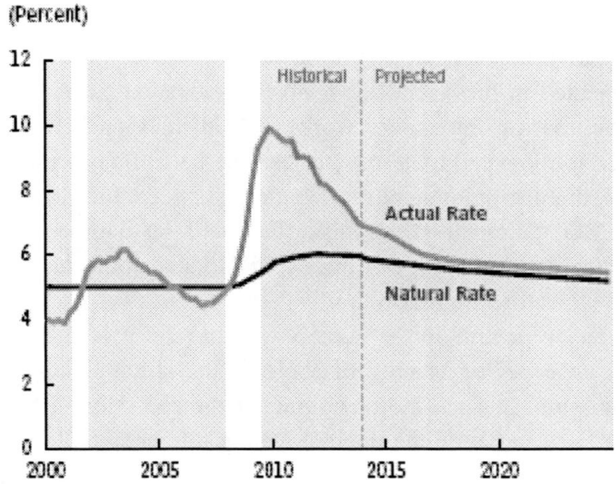

Sources: Congressional Budget Office; Bureau of Labor Statistics.

Notes: The unemployment rate is a measure of the number of jobless people who are available for and actively seeking work, expressed as a percentage of the labor force. The natural rate is CBO's estimate of the unemployment rate arising from all sources except fluctuations in aggregate demand. Data are quarterly. Historical data are plotted through 2013; projections are plotted through 2024.

Figure 10. Actual and Natural Rates of Unemployment.

CBO's labor market projections are constructed to lie in the middle of the distribution of possible outcomes, given the fiscal policies embodied in current law. Those projections are subject to many sources of uncertainty, and the outcomes could differ substantially from the projections.

Unemployment Rates

CBO expects the unemployment rate to decline over the next decade (see Figure 10), reflecting changes in cyclical and structural factors that have raised the unemployment rate since the beginning of the recession. The agency anticipates that, under current law, the unemployment rate will decline from the average of 7.0 percent in the fourth quarter of 2013, to 5.8 percent in the fourth quarter of 2017, and to 5.5 percent in 2024. The natural rate of unemployment is projected to decline from an estimated 6.0 percent at the end of 2013 to 5.6 percent in the fourth quarter of 2017 and to 5.2 percent in 2024— 0.2 percentage points above its prerecession level.[22]

The projected decline in the unemployment rate through the end of 2017 reflects primarily the expected continued economic expansion, because the increase projected in the overall demand for goods and services will create a need for businesses to hire more workers. With the gap between actual and potential GDP anticipated to narrow to just one-half of a percent in the second half of 2017, the unemployment rate would be expected to drop considerably. However, CBO anticipates that this effect will be dampened because the improvement in labor market conditions will induce some of the people who have left the labor force to return to it.

The projected decline in the unemployment rate through the end of 2017 also reflects an expected waning of some of the structural factors that have raised unemployment since the beginning of the recession. The effect of the extension of UI benefits on the unemployment rate essentially ended with the expiration of that extension at the close of 2013. And the effect of unusually large problems in matching unemployed workers with available jobs—estimated at about one-half percentage point in late 2013—is expected to recede almost entirely by 2017 (and to disappear by 2018). In contrast, the effects of stigma and erosion of skills—also estimated to have raised the unemployment rate by about one-half of a percentage point in late 2013—will continue to hamper the ability of the long-term unemployed who remain in the labor force to find work.

The projection of the small additional decline in the unemployment rate over the 2018–2024 period stems from CBO's anticipation that the effects of stigma and skill erosion will wane as more of the long-term unemployed either leave the labor force or find jobs. Even in 2024, however, CBO expects that those effects will boost the unemployment rate by about one-quarter of a percentage point.

CBO projects that the unemployment rate will be about one-quarter of a percentage point above the natural rate in the latter part of the coming decade. That gap is not based on a forecast of specific cyclical movements in the economy; instead, it is based on CBO's estimate that the unemployment rate has been, on average, higher than the natural rate since 1947 and, notably, during each of the past five business cycles. The difference arises because the shortfalls in output relative to CBO's estimate of potential output during economic downturns have been larger and more frequent than the excesses during economic expansions.

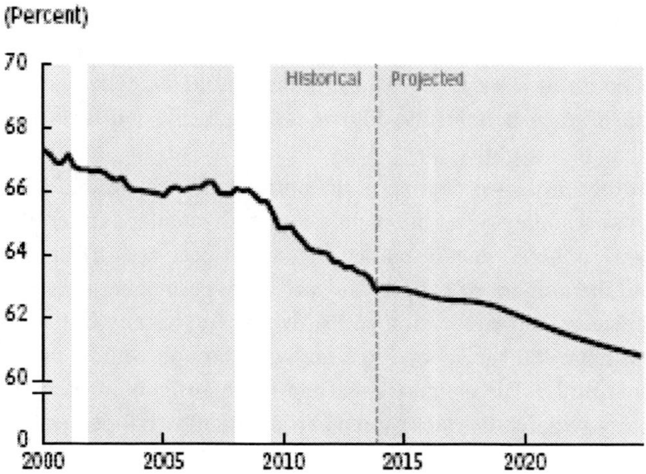

Sources: Congressional Budget Office; Bureau of Labor Statistics.

Notes: The rate of participation in the labor force is the percentage of the civilian noninstitutionalized population age 16 or older that is either working or available for and actively seeking work. Data are quarterly. Historical data are plotted through 2013; projections are plotted through 2024.

Figure 11. Historical and Projected Rate of Participation in the Labor Force.

Labor Force Participation

CBO projects that the labor force participation rate, which averaged 62.9 percent in the fourth quarter of 2013, will be at the same level, on average, in 2014 but will fall to 62.5 percent by the end of 2017 and to 60.8 percent by the end of 2024 (see Figure 11).

For 2014 to 2017, CBO anticipates that many of the people who left the labor force because of a lack of job opportunities will return as labor market conditions improve and that the number of people who stay out of the labor force (for example, to attend school) will diminish. However, CBO expects, the cyclical recovery in participation will be more than offset by the downward pressure on participation stemming from other changes. The most significant effect will come from the aging of the population (and other demographic changes), but federal tax and spending policies will also play a role. The

Affordable Care Act (ACA) will tend to reduce participation, with the largest impact stemming from new subsidies that reduce the cost of health insurance purchased through exchanges.[23] Specifically, by providing subsidies that decline with rising income (and increase with falling income) and by making some people financially better off, the ACA will create an incentive for some people to choose to work less.[24] The structure of the tax code—in which rising incomes push some people into higher tax brackets—will also reduce labor force participation slightly.

The further projected decline in the participation rate after 2017 primarily reflects the ongoing aging of the population, with smaller further effects of the federal fiscal policies just discussed. Those effects are offset in part by a reduction in the number of people who will have permanently stopped looking for work because of the recession and slow recovery; many of them would, by that period, have left the labor force anyway through retirement or by some other means. Still, CBO estimates that the lasting effects of the recession and slow recovery will depress labor force participation by 0.4 percentage points in 2024.

Employment

CBO's projections for the growth of employment during the next decade reflect the agency's projections of growth in the population and of the changes in the rate of labor force participation and the unemployment rate, described above.

Under current law, CBO expects, nonfarm employment will increase by about 7 million from the end of 2013 to the end of 2017. That gain reflects a recovery in the demand for goods and services that will boost both labor force participation and businesses' demand for labor as well as a gradual decline in the natural rate of unemployment as mismatches in the job market return to prerecession rates. Working in the opposite direction are demographic changes that will lower labor force participation. All told, CBO projects, the employmentto-population ratio will only edge upward, reaching 58.9 percent at the end of 2017—just 0.4 percentage points above the ratio at the end of 2013 and well below the peak of 63.3 percent reached at the end of 2006 and the beginning of 2007, before the recession (see Figure 12).

After 2017, the growth of employment slows somewhat more in CBO's projections, as demographic changes continue to push the labor force participation rate downward. CBO anticipates that, under current law, the employment-to-population ratio will fall to 57.5 percent in 2024.

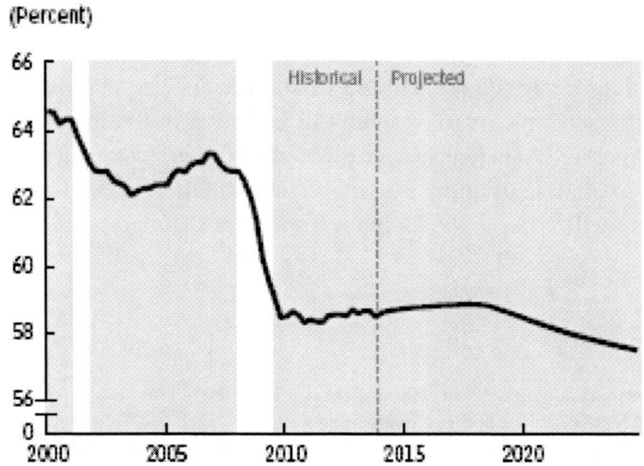

Sources: Congressional Budget Office; Bureau of Labor Statistics.

Notes: Data show the number of employed workers (as measured by the Current Population Survey) as a percentage of the civilian noninstitutionalized population age 16 or older. Data are quarterly. Historical data are plotted through 2013; projections are plotted through 2024.

Figure 12. Historical and Projected Share of the Population That Is Employed.

Uncertainty of Projections

CBO's labor market projections are subject to many sources of uncertainty. In keeping with its usual practices, CBO constructed its latest projections to lie within what it judges to be the middle of the distribution of possible outcomes, given the policies embodied in current law. Actual outcomes undoubtedly will differ from those projections in at least some respects.

One source of uncertainty regarding projections of the labor market concerns the growth in overall demand for goods and services. If demand increases more quickly or slowly than CBO projects, the labor market also will improve more quickly or slowly.

Another source of uncertainty derives from the natural rate of unemployment. If it is above CBO's estimates, future employment and output will tend to be lower, but if the natural rate is lower than CBO's estimates, future employment and output will tend to be higher.

A further source of uncertainty concerns the rate of labor force participation. One challenge in predicting that rate lies in interpreting how much of the decline in participation since 2007 will be reversed as labor market conditions improve. If more of the decline is permanent than CBO estimates, for example, employment will be lower in the long run than CBO projects. Another challenge lies in projecting the effect of the ACA on participation; if that legislation has more or less effect than CBO estimates, employment will differ in the long run from what CBO projects.

End Notes

[1] See Congressional Budget Office, The Budget and Economic Outlook: 2014 to 2024 (February 2014), Chapter 2, www.cbo.gov/publication/45010.

[2] The labor force consists of people age 16 or older in the civilian noninstitutionalized population who have jobs or who are available for and actively seeking work. People are considered unemployed if they have no work but are available for and actively seeking work.

[3] Those figures are based on data from the Bureau of Labor Statistics as of January 10, 2014; they do not account for benchmark revisions scheduled for February 7, 2014. In a preliminary announcement, the Bureau of Labor Statistics, which calculates payroll employment on the basis of a survey of nonfarm establishments, indicated that the March 2013 employment figure would probably be revised upward by about 350,000 and that the revision is more than fully accounted for by a change in the classification of some establishments providing nonmedical home-based services for the elderly and people with disabilities. With that change excluded, the growth of employment between March 2012 and March 2013 is expected to be revised downward by about 125,000. Estimates of employment growth since March 2013 also may be revised.

[4] The employment-to-population ratio uses a measure of employment from the Bureau of Labor Statistics' household survey of employment. Although the magnitudes of that measure and of payroll employment differ, their growth rates are generally similar.

[5] One manifestation of the weakness in the growth of labor compensation is the unusually large number of workers who have received no wage increases since the end of the recession. Had it not been for employers' reluctance to cut employees' nominal wages, the growth of labor compensation probably would have slowed even more. For more information, see Mary C. Daly and Bart Hobijn, Downward Nominal Wage Rigidities Bend the Philips Curve, Working Paper 2013-08 (Federal Reserve Bank of San Francisco, June 2013), http://tinyurl.com/oomgxn7.

[6] In principle, GDI equals GDP in that each dollar of production produces a dollar of income; in practice, the two differ because of difficulties in measuring both quantities. CBO defines labor income as the sum of employees' compensation and a percentage of proprietors' income (that percentage being employees' compensation as a share of the difference between GDI and proprietors' income). For further discussion, see Congressional Budget Office, How CBO Projects Income (July 2013), www.cbo.gov/publication/44433; and

Congressional Budget Office, The Budget and Economic Outlook: 2014 to 2024 (February 2014), Chapter 2, www.cbo.gov/publication/40510.

[7] Domestic economic profits are corporations' U.S. profits adjusted to remove distortions in depreciation allowances that result from tax rules and to exclude the effects of inflation on the value of inventories. Domestic economic profits exclude certain types of income that U.S.-based multinational corporations derive from foreign sources, most of which does not generate corporate income tax receipts in the United States.

[8] An alternative perspective on the increase in the unemployment rate since 2007 is offered in Casey B. Mulligan, The Expanding Social Safety Net, Working Paper 17654 (National Bureau of Economic Research, December 2011), www.nber.org/papers/ w17654, which asserts that various changes in federal policies since 2007—such as extensions of unemployment insurance— increased the effective tax rate on labor income and thereby were primarily responsible for the sharp increase in unemployment during the recession and have slowed the subsequent recovery in the labor market. See also Casey B. Mulligan, The Redistribution Recession: How Labor Market Distortions Contracted the Economy (Oxford University Press, 2012). For an opposite view, see Jesse Rothstein, "The Labor Market Four Years into the Crisis: Assessing Structural Explanations," Industrial and Labor Relations Review, vol. 65, no. 3 (March 2012), pp. 467–500, http:// tinyurl.com/ppan3j3.

[9] That roughly 4 percent shortfall is the difference between the estimate of GDP produced by the Bureau of Economic Analysis (BEA) and CBO's current estimate of potential GDP. BEA's estimate was released on January 30, 2014, after CBO completed its projection. According to BEA's release, GDP in the fourth quarter of 2013 was greater than what CBO had projected. Incorporating that higher level of GDP would probably raise CBO's estimate of potential output, but only slightly.

[10] For use in its analysis of potential output, CBO also estimates an underlying long-term rate of unemployment that incorporates only long-lasting structural factors (discussed below). CBO uses its estimate of the natural rate to analyze inflation, among other purposes; for any actual unemployment rate, a higher natural rate is an indication that employers have more difficulty hiring workers, so growth in wages will tend to be higher and upward pressure on inflation will be greater.

[11] For a more detailed discussion of the structural factors and related estimates for an earlier period, see Congressional Budget Office, Understanding and Responding to Persistently High Unemployment (February 2012), www.cbo.gov/publication/42989.

[12]. Recent research offers a variety of views on the structural factors that explain the shift in the Beveridge curve. For example, one report focuses on a combination of less efficient matching of job seekers with employers in the labor market, the effects of extensions of UI benefits on the incentives to look for work, and other factors; see Mary C. Daly and others, "A Search and Matching Approach to Labor Markets: Did the Natural Rate of Unemployment Rise?" Journal of Economic Perspectives, vol. 26, no. 3 (Summer 2012), pp. 3–26, http://tinyurl.com/olxa6b4. Other research, however, indicates that the increase in the number of the long-term unemployed accounted for the entire shift in the curve (either directly or through the effects of extensions of UI benefits); see Rand Ghayad and William Dickens, What Can We Learn by Disaggregating the Unemployment–Vacancy Relationship? Public Policy Brief 12-3 (Federal Reserve Bank of Boston, October 2012), http://tinyurl.com/qjbnv2s.

[13]. Some researchers have found that employers are less likely to respond to a résumé from an applicant who has been unemployed for more than six months than to an otherwise identical résumé from an applicant who has been unemployed for a shorter period. See, for example,

Rand Ghayad, "The Jobless Trap" (draft, 2013), http://tinyurl.com/ob6laqz (PDF, 733 KB); and Kory Kroft, Fabian Lange, and Matthew J. Notowidigdo, Duration Dependence and Labor Market Conditions: Theory and Evidence From a Field Experiment, Working Paper 18387 (National Bureau of Economic Research, September 2012), www.nber.org/papers/w18387. See also Martin Biewen and Susanne Steffes, "Unemployment Persistence: Is There Evidence for Stigma Effects?" Economic Letters, vol. 106, no. 3 (March 2010), pp. 188–190, http://tinyurl.com/pwumhpl; and Marianne Bertrand, Claudia Goldin, and Lawrence F. Katz, "Dynamics of the Gender Gap for Young Professionals in the Financial and Corporate Sectors," American Economic Journal: Applied Economics, vol. 2, no. 3 (July 2010), pp. 228–255, http://tinyurl.com/nh94ysq.

[14] See Steven J. Davis, R. Jason Faberman, and John C. Haltiwanger, Recruiting Intensity During and After the Great Recession: National and Industry Evidence, Working Paper 17782 (National Bureau of Economic Research, January 2012), www.nber.org/papers/ w17782.

[15] In addition, lawmakers enacted other temporary provisions to aid the unemployed, including special provisions that made it easier for states to pay benefits under the extended benefits program (from February 2009 through December 2013) and a weekly supplement of $25 that was available to people receiving regular, emergency, and extended benefits (from February 2009 through December 2010).

[16] Such benefits have been the subject of research for several decades. A widely cited publication from 1990 shows that eligibility for an extra five weeks of benefits led, on average, to a one-week increase in the duration of unemployment; see Lawrence F. Katz and Bruce D. Meyer, "The Impact of the Potential Duration of Unemployment Benefits on the Duration of Unemployment," Journal of Public Economics, vol. 41, no. 1 (February 1990), pp. 45–72, http://tinyurl.com/qyw7elf. A more recent publication suggests that most of that effect represented an expanded search effort, which ultimately could result in better matching of workers and jobs; see Raj Chetty, "Moral Hazard Versus Liquidity and Optimal Unemployment Insurance," Journal of Political Economy, vol. 116, no. 2 (April 2008), pp. 173–234, http://tinyurl.com/ ozfs7uq. Most research focusing on the extension of benefits in recent years has revealed smaller effects and indicated that much of the increase in unemployment duration was among people who would otherwise have left the labor force, thus indicating that the increase in duration did not imply a decrease in employment. See Rob Valletta and Katherine Kuang, Extended Unemployment and UI Benefits, Economic Letter 2010-12 (Federal Reserve Bank of San Francisco, April 2010), http://tinyurl.com/mtfpx6j; Jesse Rothstein "Unemployment Insurance and Job Search in the Great Recession," Brookings Papers on Economic Activity (Fall 2011), pp. 142–196, http://tinyurl.com/qgtgcuj; and Henry Farber and Robert G. Valletta, Do Extended Unemployment Benefits Lengthen Unemployment Spells? Evidence From Recent Cycles in the U.S. Labor Market, Working Paper 19048 (National Bureau of Economic Research, May 2013), www.nber.org/papers/w19048. In contrast, a preliminary study reports large negative effects on employment from the extension of benefits in recent years, reflecting employers' responses to an increase in prevailing wages (albeit a relatively small one) that was necessary to attract UI beneficiaries to accept jobs. See Marcus Hagedorn and others, Unemployment Benefits and Unemployment in the Great Recession: The Role of Macro Effects, Working Paper 19499 (National Bureau of Economic Research, October 2013), www.nber.org/papers/ w19499.

[17] See Congressional Budget Office, letter to the Honorable Chris Van Hollen concerning the ways in which extending certain unemployment benefits would affect output and employment in 2014 (December 3, 2013), www.cbo.gov/publication/44929.

[18] For further discussion about underlying trends in labor force participation rates by age and by sex, see Congressional Budget Office, CBO's Labor Force Projections Through 2021 (March 2011), www.cbo.gov/publication/22011.

[19] See Courtney C. Coile and Phillip B. Levine, "The Market Crash and Mass Layoffs: How the Current Economic Crisis May Affect Retirement," B.E. Journal of Economic Analysis and Policy, vol. 11, no. 1 (April 2011), http://tinyurl.com/p6uqspw.

[20] See Congressional Budget Office, Policy Options for the Social Security Disability Insurance Program (July 2012), www.cbo.gov/ publication/43421.

[21] For further discussion of economic projections through 2024, see Congressional Budget Office, The Budget and Economic Outlook: 2014 to 2024 (February 2014), Chapter 2, www.cbo.gov/ publication/45010.

[22] For use in its analysis of potential output, CBO also estimates an underlying long-term rate of unemployment that incorporates only long-lasting structural factors. Of the three structural factors discussed in this report, only the stigma and erosion of skills related to the long-term unemployed are expected to be sufficiently long lasting to be included in that underlying longterm rate. Thus, CBO estimates that the underlying long-term rate of unemployment was 5.0 percent before the recession, that it rose to 5.5 percent in 2013, that it will remain there through 2017 because the effects of stigma and skill erosion will remain roughly constant over the next four years, and that it will then decline to 5.2 percent in 2024 as those effects wane.

[23] As referred to in this report, the ACA comprises the Patient Protection and Affordable Care Act, the health care provisions of the Health Care and Education Reconciliation Act of 2010, and the effects of subsequent judicial decisions, statutory changes, and administrative actions.

[24] For more information, see Congressional Budget Office, The Budget and Economic Outlook: 2014 to 2024 (February 2014), Appendix C, www.cbo.gov/publication/45010.

In: Labor Market Recovery …
Editor: Kyla C. Sims

ISBN: 978-1-63117-890-0
© 2014 Nova Science Publishers, Inc.

Chapter 2

THE INCREASE IN UNEMPLOYMENT SINCE 2007: IS IT CYCLICAL OR STRUCTURAL?*

Linda Levine

SUMMARY

The unemployment rate greatly increased after the onset of the latest recession in December 2007, when it measured 5.0%. The rate peaked at 10.0% in October 2009, four months after the recession's official end in June 2009. More than three years into the recovery, the unemployment rate averaged 8.1% in 2012. Given its still elevated level, policymakers may continue to be concerned about how to spur economic growth and create jobs.

Over the past few years, Congress has used fiscal policy and the Federal Reserve (Fed) has used monetary policy to put the economy on a path toward the level of demand for goods and services that preceded the 2007-2009 recession. Firms react to recessions by laying off workers, and the deeper the downturn in the business cycle, the greater the rise in unemployment that results. Expansionary fiscal and monetary policies commonly have been used to remedy what is known as cyclical unemployment.

---

* This is an edited, reformatted and augmented version of Congressional Research Service Publication, No. R41785, dated January 24, 2013.

The unemployment rate has not been as responsive as had been hoped to the countercyclical measures undertaken by Congress and the Fed. Consequently, some have suggested that an increase in another type of unemployment—referred to as structural unemployment—has accounted for much of the rise in the unemployment rate from pre-recession levels. These observers assert that the rise in unemployment due to change in the structure of the economy represents "a new normal" of elevated unemployment rates for years to come.

Structural unemployment develops for different reasons than cyclical unemployment. Structural unemployment results when jobseekers do not move quickly into vacant jobs. Obstacles that lengthen the spell of unemployment (i.e., prolong the period of job search) include mismatches between the skills or locations of jobless workers and the skill requirements or locations of available jobs. Another impediment is the composition of the unemployed, such as more workers whose connection to their former employers is permanently severed (i.e., fewer workers likely to be recalled from layoffs once business revives at their former employers). A third factor that may contribute to long-term unemployment is known as labor market institutions, such as unemployment benefit programs.

The measures enacted by Congress have chiefly focused on alleviating cyclical unemployment. To the extent that the still-high unemployment rate results from the slow pace of output growth during the recovery, economic theory suggests that fiscal and monetary stimulus would be suitable strategies for further reducing joblessness. To the extent that structural factors have contributed to the still-high unemployment rate, economic theory suggests measures such as promoting the education and retraining of workers who permanently lost jobs in hard-hit industries (e.g., home building) so that they can acquire the skills needed to obtain employment in other industries.

This report assesses the relative magnitudes of cyclical and structural unemployment as they respond to different policy measures. An analysis of changes since 2007 in a variety of labor market indicators across industries and areas finds patterns that strongly suggest most of the increase in the U.S. unemployment rate is cyclical (i.e., due to depressed aggregate demand). Empirical studies suggest that, although structural unemployment has temporarily increased, it accounted for a minority of the rise in the unemployment rate in recent years.

Introduction

During the past few years, economists have been debating how much of the increase in unemployment since the start of the 2007-2009 recession is due to reduced demand for goods and services compared with compositional changes entailing worker reallocation across industries and areas.[1] In other words, how much of the increase in the official unemployment rate from 5.0% at the recession's outset in December 2007 to a peak of 10.0% in October 2009 was cyclical unemployment and how much was structural unemployment?

Distinguishing cyclical from structural unemployment is more than an academic exercise. Their relative contribution to the increase in the unemployment rate since 2007 has different implications for the pace at which the economy can grow without spurring inflation and for which public policies are most appropriate to lower an unemployment rate that remains elevated long after the latest recession's end in June 2009.

Many workers who became unemployed during the 2007-2009 recession are expected to return to jobs in their former industries as demand for the goods and services they previously produced grows during the recovery phase of the business cycle. Fiscal and monetary policies often have been used to jump-start aggregate demand and job growth for the cyclically unemployed. In response to the latest recession, for example, recent Congresses enacted multiple measures to stimulate demand and promote job creation while the Federal Reserve (Fed) undertook various strategies to mitigate the financial crisis that coincided with the recession and to stimulate economic activity.[2] If the increase in unemployment is largely due to the sluggish pace of output growth since the recession's end, then economic theory suggests that fiscal and monetary stimulus would be suitable strategies for lowering the unemployment rate from its still-elevated average of 8.1% in 2012.

Those workers who permanently lost their jobs during the 2007-2009 recession are expected to experience a longer spell of unemployment than those temporarily laid off until product demand revives in their former sectors of employment. The duration of job losers' unemployment may be further lengthened if the skills they possess do not match the skills required by jobs in growing sectors or if they live in areas different from those experiencing job growth. To overcome skill mismatch for example, displaced workers may require retraining or additional formal education. Congress recognized that different public policies are appropriate for helping structurally unemployed workers return to economically productive activities when it included training provisions among the countercyclical measures in the American Recovery and Reinvestment Act, for example.[3]

Rather than persisting in their search for jobs, some structurally unemployed workers may drop out of the labor force, thereby reducing the supply of labor and the capacity of the economy to grow in the long run.[4] A smaller labor force also reduces income tax payments and imposes additional costs on society. For example, because older workers, the partially disabled and less educated are among those most likely to stop participating in the labor force, early claiming of Society Security retirement benefits and entering the Social Security Disability Income program could increase.[5]

Given the different implications of cyclical and structural unemployment for policymakers, this report distinguishes between the relative magnitude of the two in recent years. Before conducting this analysis, the report defines a few concepts that will help the reader navigate the remainder of the report.

A Few Concepts Briefly Explained

Economists often break down unemployment into three types: frictional, structural, and cyclical.

- *Frictional* unemployment arises from the ever-present movement of people into and out of jobs. Examples include the unemployment of college graduates while searching for their first jobs, of family caregivers returning to the labor force, and of workers who quit jobs before having found new ones. Both frictional and structural unemployment involve the worker-to-job matching process. Two distinctions between them are the voluntary nature of some frictional unemployment and its shorter duration compared with structural unemployment.
- *Structural* unemployment arises from obstacles to the worker-to-job-matching process that lengthen unemployment spells. Impediments to unemployed workers quickly moving to firms with available jobs include mismatches (between the skills or locations of jobless workers and the skill requirements or locations of available jobs), the composition of the unemployed (toward workers who permanently lost jobs vis-a-vis workers temporarily laid off, for example), and the characteristics of labor market institutions (such as the wage-replacement rate and duration of unemployment benefits).
- *Cyclical* unemployment arises when the economy experiences a decrease in the demand for goods and services. Employers adjust to a downturn in the business cycle by temporarily laying off workers and cutting the hours of employees retained to fill reduced product

> demand. When demand starts to revive, firms may be reluctant to immediately resume hiring and may first increase the hours of their existing work force. Once firms feel confident that economic growth will continue, they recall the experienced workers laid off during the recession.

Under certain conditions, however, cyclical unemployment may evolve into structural unemployment. If the economy grows slowly for an extended period after a recession's end and causes the unemployment rate to remain high for quite some time, then some of what began as cyclical unemployment may become structural unemployment. The following is an example of how this occurs. By definition, the skills of the cyclically unemployed at the outset of their displacement match the skills demanded by employers. But the longer these workers remain jobless, the greater the likelihood their skills will become rusty. As economic growth strengthens and firms start hiring workers, the skills of the long-term unemployed may have so deteriorated that they no longer match the skill requirements of available jobs.

Frictional, structural, and cyclical unemployment are not directly measured, but policy analysts have estimated the nonaccelerating inflation rate of unemployment (NAIRU). Because the NAIRU is estimated without regard to fluctuations in aggregate demand (i.e., without regard to the business cycle), it commonly is used as a proxy for the structural unemployment rate. The NAIRU or natural rate of unemployment reflects the extent of long-term slack in the labor market, which is helpful to know when formulating policy. For example, a substantial increase in structural unemployment implies that there is much less excess labor (capacity) in the economy. Consequently, the Fed cannot reduce the official unemployment rate as much as it previously could without raising the inflation rate.

CYCLICAL VS. STRUCTURAL UNEMPLOYMENT

Based on the following analysis of changes in multiple labor market indicators by industry and area, a majority of the increase in unemployment between the 2007-2009 recession's onset and its peak in 2010 appears to be cyclical. As discussed in detail below, this finding is supported by several empirical studies which estimated that any increase in structural unemployment that occurred accounted for a minority of the rise in the U.S.

unemployment rate. The results do not suggest that the nation is facing a "new normal" of elevated unemployment rates for years to come.

Evidence of Greatly Increased Cyclical Unemployment

> The mismatch argument for sustained increases in the unemployment rate and the NAIRU is predicated on imbalances in labor supply and demand across sectors and skill groups. The extent of such imbalances can be assessed by examining employment growth and unemployment rates across industry sectors, states, and occupations.[6]

This approach is pursued below using annual average data from 2007 to 2010, the year in which the unemployment rate peaked at 9.6%.

Job Loss by Industry and Unemployment Rates by State

The 7.8 million jobs lost between 2007 and 2010 occurred across a broad swath of industries.[7] The number of jobs on employers' payrolls plummeted in 18 of the 24 industries shown in **Figure 1**. Cyclically sensitive industries, such as manufacturing and construction, bore the brunt of job losses during the latest recession just as they did during prior recessions. When aggregate employment stopped declining in March 2010, "the dispersion of employment gains and losses across sectors returned to its pre-recession level, suggesting very little imbalance in the pace of employment growth at that point."[8]

The data displayed in **Figure 1** support DeLong's statement that "What we have witnessed is not a shift in demand into sectors lacking an adequate number of qualified and productive workers, but rather a collapse in the level of aggregate demand."[9] He concluded that, as of fall 2010, evidence was lacking of "labor shortages, rising wages, and increasing prices in expanding sectors, accompanied by high unemployment elsewhere in the economy," which would be the case if skills mismatch was the major explanation for the nation's high unemployment rate. DeLong went on to note, however, that were unemployment to remain high "for two or three more years" then structural unemployment could well become a bigger factor because "nothing converts cyclical unemployment into structural unemployment more certainly than prolonged unemployment."

Just as job losses occurred in most industries between 2007 and 2010, so too did the unemployment rate rise in every state in the nation.[10] The across-the-board increase in unemployment rates suggests that labor demand fell throughout the country, belying the notion of a mismatch between the locations of available jobs and workers desiring employment.

Only two states—Alaska (6,500 jobs) and North Dakota (17,200 jobs)—and the District of Columbia (17,100 jobs) posted net employment gains between 2007 and 2010.[11] This implies that unemployed workers had little incentive to move to find jobs, which does not support speculation that conditions in the housing market dampened the migration rate of unemployed homeowners.

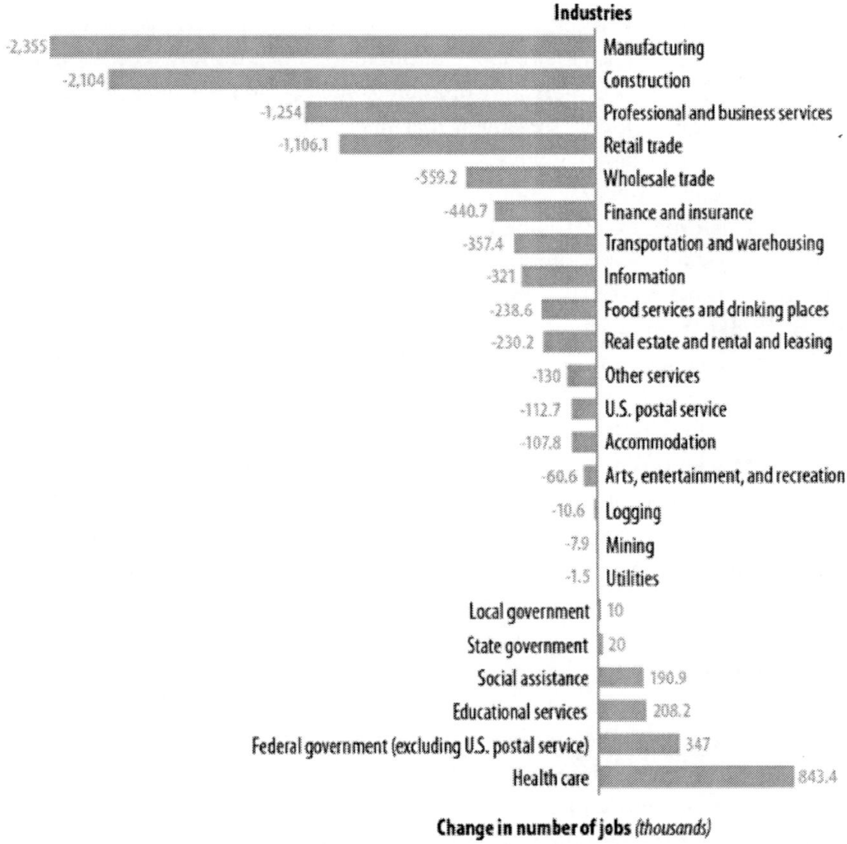

Source: Created by CRS from the total number of nonfarm jobs in 2007 and 2010, according to U.S. Bureau of Labor Statistics data from the Current Employment Statistics program.

Figure 1. Change in the Number of Jobs by Industry, 2007-2010.

Most empirical analyses also suggest that the state of the housing market is not an especially good explanation for the decrease in geographic mobility since 2007.[12] Molloy, Smith, and Wozniak found neither the housing market contraction nor the 2007-2009 recession to be persuasive reasons for the recent decrease in internal migration rates.[13] Kaplan and Schulhofer-Wohl determined that the large drop in annual interstate migration rates starting in 2006, which had led some observers to infer a connection to "house lock," was instead the result of a change in the Census Bureau's procedure for imputing missing data in the Current Population Survey (CPS). Kaplan and Schulhofer-Wohl considered the smaller change in migration rates from two other sources (the Census Bureau's American Community Survey and the Internal Revenue Service) to bolster their assessment that interstate migration has not recently decreased to a substantial degree.[14]

Using data from yet another source (the Census Bureau's Survey of Income and Program Participation), Aaronson and Davis estimated that the decrease in state-to-state migration rates during the 2007-2009 recession and the first year of recovery were similar for homeowners and renters and also were similar to their experience during prior recessions. They further found little empirical support for the house lock argument based on the severity of a state's decline in housing prices or the unemployment status of the head of homeowner households.[15]

Schmitt and Warner took a different approach to determining whether differences in housing market conditions by state affected the geographic mobility of job losers. They estimated that the probability of displaced workers' moving over the 2007-2009 period was little affected by differences in housing market performance across states.[16] Displaced workers in Nevada, California, Florida, Arizona, and Michigan—which were among the 10 states to experience the largest decreases in a statewide housing price index—had almost the same likelihood of not moving after losing their jobs (90.7%) as displaced workers in the 10 states with the best housing markets (91.5%).[17]

Using monthly microdata from the Current Population Survey and an econometric model, Valletta found no evidence in favor of the house-lock argument. Because house lock would mean a longer period of job search in the local labor market for owners of homes whose values had decreased, he examined differences in unemployment durations between homeowners and renters across metropolitan areas differentiated by their degree of decreases in home prices. The results of his analysis do not support the hypothesis that reduced geographic mobility among homeowners contributed to high unemployment during the recession and through 2011.[18]

Alternatively, based on their construction of a model of metropolitan area housing and labor markets and migration, Karahan and Rhee concluded that house lock reduced geographic mobility and exacerbated the increase in unemployment during the Great (2007-2009) Recession.[19] They estimated that, absent the housing bust, workers would have been more likely to move during the recession from areas with higher to lower unemployment rates (the migration rate would have risen). As a result, the decline in migration shown in the various data sources referenced above understated the impact of the sharp drop in house prices on worker mobility and unemployment. Geographic mismatch resulting from the housing bust may explain about 0.5 percentage points of the increase in the unemployment rate during the 2007-2009 recession, according to Karahan and Rhee.

Underemployment by Industry

Firms can adjust the quantity of labor they use in response to a decrease in aggregate demand not only by reducing the size of their work forces but also by cutting the hours of qualified employees they retain on their payrolls. The latter action produces "underemployment," that is, workers employed part-time who would prefer to be employed full-time but cannot for economic reasons (e.g., unfavorable business conditions).[20] Because underemployment reflects the demand for workers who possess the skills required to perform their jobs, analysis of changes in underemployment takes skill mismatch out of the equation.

The demand for qualified employees fell across every industry shown in **Figure 2**. The total number of underemployed workers slightly more than doubled over the three-year period to 8.9 million in 2010, when the unemployment rate reached its most recent peak.[21] Underemployment increased even more so in the following diverse group of industries: retail trade; social assistance; food services and drinking places; health care; accommodation; arts, entertainment, and recreation; educational services; and state government.

Jayadev and Konczal analyzed the trend in underemployment from 2000 to 2010 for the construction and financial activities industries, and for all other industries. They found that the number of persons involuntarily working fewer than 35 hours a week had about doubled for both the construction and financial activities industries and for all other industries since the outset of the 2007-2009 recession, which coincided with a financial crisis related to the collapse of the housing market. Jayadev and Konczal took this as "a sign that underemployment is hitting every sector, not just those with hangovers from the bubble."[22] In other words, they believe this indicates that cyclical forces have primarily affected the labor market.

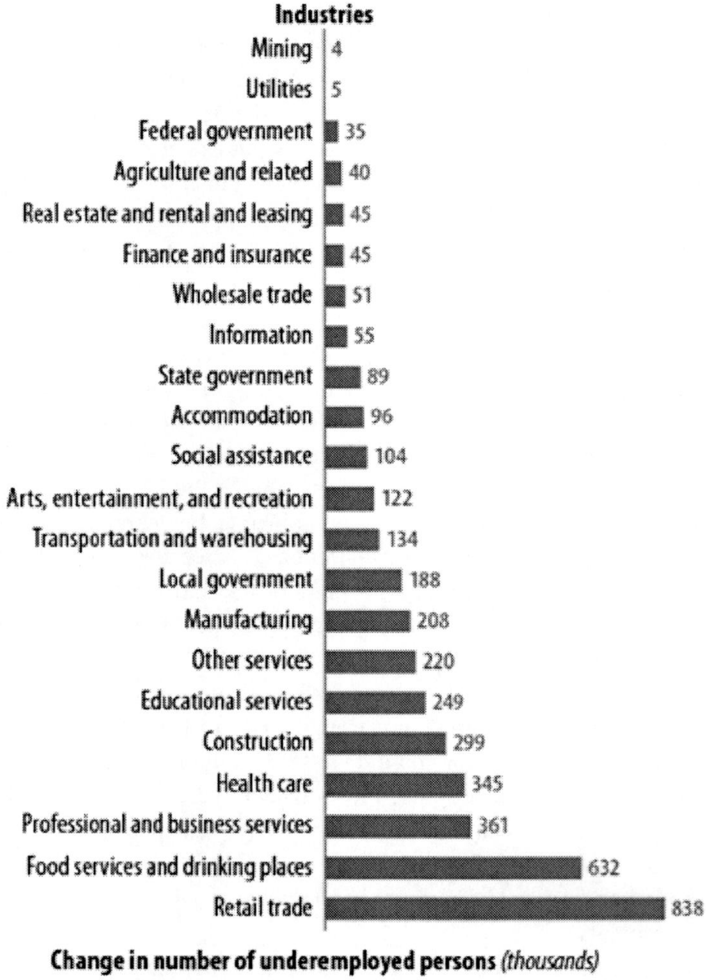

Source: Created by CRS from the total number of workers employed part-time for economic reasons in 2007 and 2010 according to U.S. Bureau of Labor Statistics data from the Current Population Survey.

Notes: Underemployed workers want to work full time but are working part-time (1-34 hours a week) for an economic reason (e.g., their hours were cut back or they were unable to find full-time jobs).

Figure 2. Change in the Number of Underemployed Workers by Industry, 2007-2010.

The Hiring Rate by Industry and Region

The decrease in the hiring rate (i.e., the number of hires as a percent of total nonfarm employment) between 2007 and 2010 in almost all industries for which data are available from the Job Openings and Labor Turnover Survey (JOLTS) again suggests the primacy of cyclical over structural factors.[23] (See **Figure 3**.) Employers in less than half of these industries hired relatively more workers in 2010 than in 2009. Rates returned to pre-recession levels in only construction[24] and the federal government.[25]

Offshore outsourcing, by changing the skill mix of jobs into which U.S. workers can be hired, has been offered as a reason for the slow recovery of the labor market. The largest declines in the hiring rate between 2007 and 2010 were in industries in which the major occupations are not especially vulnerable to offshoring, however. (Offshorable occupations have been defined as those whose duties do not require in-person contact between employees and customers or those whose duties do not have to be performed in the United States.)[26] Cooks, food preparation and serving workers (including fast food), and waiters and waitresses are among the leading occupations in the accommodations and food services industry, in which the hiring rate plunged 27.6 percentage points as shown in **Figure 3**.[27] Amusement and recreation attendants, fitness trainers and aerobics instructors, and landscaping and groundskeeping workers account for the largest shares of workers in the arts, entertainment and recreation industry, which experienced the second biggest decrease in the rate of hires. Counter and rental clerks; general maintenance and repair workers; property, real estate, and community association managers; and real estate sales agents are among the leading occupations in the real estate and rental and leasing industry, just as cashiers, retail salespersons, stock clerks, and order fillers are in the retail trade industry. Although some jobs in the finance and insurance industry may be more vulnerable to offshoring than the aforementioned jobs in industries whose hiring rate fell most precipitously between 2007 and 2010, tellers—a non-offshorable occupation—comprise the largest share of the finance and insurance industry's employment.

Just as hiring activity fell in most industries between 2007 and 2010, so too did hires drop in all four geographic areas for which JOLTS data are available. The West and South recorded the largest declines in the hiring rate (i.e., each fell by 11.7 percentage points to 36.1% and 37.3%, respectively).[28] Both regions include states that are among the most hard hit by the end of the housing bubble (e.g., Nevada and Florida). In the Midwest, the hiring rate decreased by 8.5 percentage points to 36.9% in 2010.[29] The Northeast's rate fell the least over the three-year period, decreasing by 4.7 percentage points to 34.3% in 2010.[30]

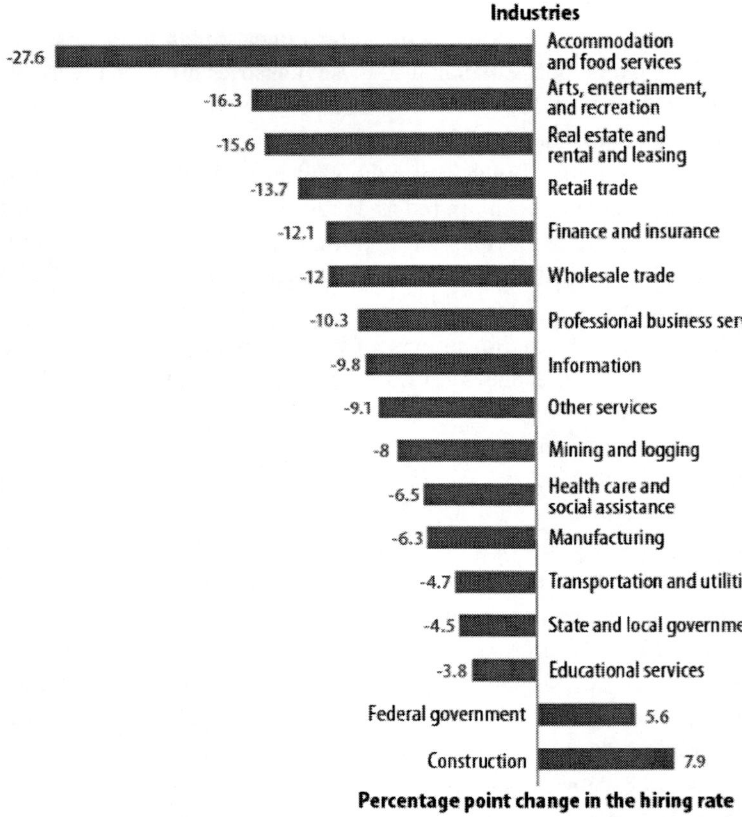

Source: Created by CRS from the hiring rate in 2007 and 2010 according to U.S. Bureau of Labor Statistics data from the Job Openings and Labor Turnover Survey.

Notes: The hiring rate is the number of hires during the entire year as a percent of annual average nonfarm employment.

Figure 3. Percentage Point Change in the Hiring Rate by Industry, 2007-2010.

The Ratio of Unemployed Workers to Job Openings by Industry

The number of unemployed workers for every job opening (vacancy) increased during the 2007- 2009 recession. From 1.8 unemployed workers per job opening at the recession's outset in December 2007, the ratio peaked at 6.7 in July 2009, one month after the recession ended.[31]

In late 2010, there were still about five unemployed workers for every job vacancy. The ratio has fallen slowly since then.[32]

With so many more jobseekers than available jobs it seems fairly straightforward for employers to transform vacancies into hires. But, the mismatch argument posits that employers are having difficulty filling vacancies because the skills unemployed workers possess do not qualify them for the available positions. The number of experienced (i.e., qualified) unemployed workers per job opening increased in every industry through 2010, however, when the unemployment rate mostly recently peaked at 9.6%.[33] (See **Table 1**.)

Sahin, Song, Topa, and Violante estimated that the rise in industry-level mismatch does not account for much of the increase in the unemployment rate and that the rise in mismatch was short-lived. Their analysis indicates that the increase in mismatch across industries explained between 0.59 and 0.75 percentage points of the rise in U.S. unemployment from its average of 4.6% in 2006, to its peak of 10.0% in October 2009, "i.e., at most 14 percent of the increase."[34] In 2010, the mismatch between unemployed workers and job vacancies across industries started moving toward pre-recession levels.

To some observers, the much higher ratio of unemployed workers to job openings in the construction industry compared with other industries in 2010 and the much higher ratio in the construction industry during the current recovery compared with the recovery from the 2001 recession suggest an increase in structural unemployment.[35] The latest recession was partly caused by the bursting of the housing bubble, before which high demand for homes drove up construction employment and likely held down the industry's ratio during the recovery from the 2001 recession.[36]

In addition, the existence of more qualified jobseekers than job openings in every industry shown in **Table 1** suggests that an economy-wide reduction in demand rather than shifts in demand across industries is the greater contributor to the increase in unemployment.

Lastly, even if many of the workers let go by residential building construction firms and residential specialty trade contractors face prolonged unemployment due to mismatch, the overall impact is likely to be limited because the two components of the construction industry accounted for only 2.4% of total nonfarm employment in 2005 (before the housing bubble burst).

Table 1. The Ratio of Experienced Unemployed Workers to Job Openings by Industry

Industry	Number of Experienced Unemployed Workers[a] Divided by Number of Job Openings[b]	
	December 2007	December 2010
Total private nonfarm industries	1.6	5.3
Mining and logging	1.3	3.7
Construction	9.7	51.4
Manufacturing	2.8	9.0
Wholesale and retail trade	1.8	7.7
Transportation and utilities	2.1	5.1
Information	1.5	3.4
Financial activities	1.2	3.0
Professional and business services	1.1	2.7
Education and health services	0.7	2.3
Leisure and hospitality	2.1	7.3
Other services	1.7	4.5
Government	1.1	2.6

Source: Calculated by CRS from Current Population Survey (CPS) and Job Openings and Labor Turnover Survey (JOLTS) data.

Notes: Comparable data on unemployment by industry from the CPS and on job openings by industry from JOLTS are available monthly on a not seasonally adjusted basis. When using not seasonally adjusted monthly data the appropriate comparison across time is month over year (e.g., December of 2007 and 2010).

[a] Experienced unemployed workers in a given industry are those workers who were employed in that industry just prior to separation from their employers. Persons who became unemployed upon entering or reentering the labor force are excluded.

[b] Job openings include only those positions for which employers are recruiting from outside their firms and for which work could start within 30 days regardless of when a suitable candidate is found.

Evidence of Somewhat Increased Structural Unemployment

Anomalies that occurred during the latest recession and ongoing recovery suggest that structural impediments to efficiently matching workers with jobs may have contributed more to the increase in the unemployment rate from 5.0% in December 2007 to a peak of 10.0% in October 2009 than they did during earlier fluctuations in the business cycle. These anomalies are the incidence of permanent job loss and of long-term unemployment as well as the nature of the relationship between unemployment and job vacancies. Most of the studies reviewed below estimated that any increase in structural unemployment in recent years accounted for a minority of the unemployment rate's rise, however. A few analyses further suggest that the recent increase in structural unemployment in the United States is unlikely to persist as occurred in some European countries starting in the 1980s and extending into the 1990s. Their conclusion that the U.S. labor market has not attained "a new normal" of high unemployment rates for years to come is partly due to the temporary nature of the Emergency Unemployment Compensation program enacted in 2008 and most recently extended by Congress through 2013.[37]

Permanent Job Loss and Long-Term Unemployment

"Two particularly worrisome signs suggestive of structural labor market problems ... are the concentration of the rise in unemployment among permanent job losers and the huge increase in long-term unemployment."[38] The unemployment rate may be higher than it otherwise would have been had the composition of unemployed workers not shifted toward the two hard-to-employ groups.

Workers who permanently lost their jobs (i.e., job losers *not* on temporary layoffs) grew from 1.7% of the labor force in 2007 to 5.1% in 2010, the year in which the unemployment rate most recently peaked.[39] In contrast, permanent job losers rose from 1.7% of the labor force in 1979 to just 4.0% in 1983 after the severe 1981-1982 recession.[40] Job losers' share of the labor force grew from 1.2% in 2000, before the start of the mild 2001 recession, to a much lower 2.6% in 2003 during the ensuing jobless recovery.

Temporary layoffs can be quickly reversed as the economy picks up steam, but job losses sever the employee-employer relationship and force job losers to search for new positions. Former employees of industries that may not soon see demand return to pre-recession levels (e.g., the residential construction industry) may experience especially lengthy unemployment if their skill sets do not match those of jobs in expanding sectors.[41]

More than six million workers were unemployed for longer than 27 weeks (i.e., the long-term unemployed) in 2010. They comprised over 40% of all workers unemployed in that and the two subsequent years. Earlier postwar peaks in the long-term unemployed's share of all unemployed workers were about half as large.[42] The long-term unemployment rate (i.e., persons unemployed more than six months as a share of the labor force) was 4.2% in 2010. At no other time during the postwar period was long-term unemployment more prevalent.[43]

Shimer estimated that the probability of reemployment decreases the longer workers remain unemployed in either good or bad economic times, but he also found that recessions result in the largest percentage decrease in the job-finding probability of the long-term unemployed.[44] Although it is unclear why the long-term unemployed have more difficulty getting jobs, some speculate that firms are reluctant to hire those toward the end of the unemployment queue because their skills may have atrophied from lack of use.[45] The long-term unemployed's chances of reemployment may also be depressed if their unemployment stigmatizes them in employers' eyes. In addition, workers may become demoralized after being jobless for a very long time and as a result, search less intensively for jobs.

Lazear and Spletzer concluded that the 11th postwar recession was not unlike earlier recessions— except more severe—with cyclical (transitory) factors largely accounting for the still-elevated unemployment rate. They noted that the high prevalence of long-term unemployment is an atypical feature of the Great Recession which "is not due to any observed structural change, but rather to the depth of the current recession."[46]

The Vacancy Rate and the Unemployment Rate

Yet a third anomaly suggestive of structural problems in the labor market is the nature of the relationship between the job vacancy (openings) rate and the unemployment rate after the recession's end in June 2009. Historically, there has been a stable negative association over the course of the business cycle between the vacancy rate (i.e., vacancies as a percentage of all filled and unfilled jobs) and the unemployment rate.[47] During economic expansions when demand is strong (i.e., the vacancy rate is high), the unemployment rate is low. During economic contractions when demand is weak (i.e., the vacancy rate is low), the unemployment rate is high.

The inverse relationship between the job openings and unemployment rates was maintained during the 2007-2009 recession, but both rates have increased during much of the recovery period. The unemployment rate averaged 2.6 percentage points higher in the January-March 2012 period than the rate predicted by their historically inverse relationship, according to Barnichon, Elsby, Hobijn and Sahin.[48] They also estimated that the higher than predicted unemployment rate was mostly due to the unusually low rate at which workers were hired to fill vacancies given the stage of the business cycle. Although the economists estimated that the shortfall in hires was present in many industries, the construction industry was found to have contributed most to the overall shortfall. Daly, Hobijn, Sahin, and Valletta suggested that if half of the unusually large number of construction workers who remain unemployed were to find jobs in other industries as the recovery proceeds, "the decline of construction would cause structural unemployment to increase by only about 0.4 percentage point."[49]

Estimates of the Increase in Structural Unemployment

Several economists estimated how much structural unemployment increased and contributed to the steep rise of the unemployment rate from a pre-recession average of 4.6% in 2007 to 9.3% in 2009 and a still higher 9.6% in 2010. Most of the empirical studies whose results are summarized in **Table 2** relied to varying degrees on recent deviations from the above-described negative relationship between vacancy and unemployment rates and from the positive relationship between the job-finding rate and the vacancy-unemployment ratio. Another difference that may affect their results is the time period covered by the analyses (e.g., ending in 2009 or 2010).

Six of the seven studies estimated an increase in structural unemployment that accounted for a minority of the recent rise in the unemployment rate. The results of these analyses imply that the increase in structural unemployment may explain between 20% and 35% (or 1.0-1.75 percentage points) of the 5 percentage point increase in the unemployment rate between 2007 and 2010.

Researchers disagree on the precise allocation of the unemployment rate's rise to skill as opposed to geographic mismatch. This likely relates in part to the different measures of mismatch they developed. Batini, Celasun, Dowling et al. estimated that their measure of skill mismatch by state raised structural unemployment by 1.0-1.75 percentage points between 2007 and 2009. (See **Table 2**.) In contrast, Estevao and Tsounta found that unfavorable conditions in the housing market (which may have reduced geographic mobility) accounted for more of their estimated 1.75 percentage point increase in structural unemployment over the 2006-2010 period than did skill mismatch (1 percentage point and 0.5 percentage point, respectively). Estevao and Tsounta estimated that the remaining rise in structural unemployment (0.25 percentage points) was due to the interaction of skill match with foreclosures. For their part, Sahin et al. found that geographic mismatch did not play a role in the unemployment rate's increase from 4.6% on average in 2006 to its October 2009 peak (10.0%), whereas mismatch across occupations explained between 0.6 and 0.9 percentage point of the rise.[50]

Table 2. Estimates of the Increase Since 2007 in the Structural Unemployment Rate

Percentage Point Increase in the Structural Unemployment Rate[a]	Author	Source
0.6-1.9, preferred estimate of 1.25	Mary Daly, Bart Hobijn, and Rob Valletta	The Recent Evolution of the Natural Rate of Unemployment, Federal Reserve Bank of San Francisco (FRBSF) Working Paper 2011-05, January 2011
1.0-1.75	Nicoletta Batini, Oya Celasun, Thomas Dowling, et al.	United States: Selected Issues Paper, International Monetary Fund, Country Report No. 10/248, July 2010
1.75	Marcello Estevao and Evridiki Tsounta	Has the Great Recession Raised U.S. Structural Unemployment?, IMF Working Paper 11/105, May 2011
1.7	Justin Weidner and John C. Williams	What Is the New Normal Unemployment Rate?, FRBSF Economic Letter 2011-05, February 14, 2011
1.5	Regis Barnichon and Andrew Figura	What Drives Movements in the Unemployment Rate?, Federal Reserve Board, Finance and Economics Discussion Series Working Paper 2010-48, August 20, 2010
2.5	Narayana Kocherlakota	Back Inside the FOMC, speech by the President of the Federal Reserve Bank of Minneapolis, September 8, 2010

Source: Created by CRS from the studies referenced in the table.

[a] There is no officially calculated rate of structural unemployment. The nonaccelerating inflation rate of unemployment (NAIRU) is a proxy for the structural unemployment rate because the NAIRU (or natural rate) is estimated without regard to fluctuations in aggregate demand.

The analysis of Herz and van Rens gave comparatively more weight to geographic than skills mismatch: they estimated that mismatch across states accounted for 0.1 percentage point of the 5 percentage point increase in unemployment during the Great Recession compared to 0.03 percentage point for skill mismatch.[51] Although Daly, Hobijn, and Valletta found that mismatch accounted for a larger share (0.5 percentage points or less) of their preferred estimated increase of 1.25 percentage points in structural unemployment from 2007 to 2010, it nonetheless explained a minority of the increase.

Empirical estimates of the impact of unemployment benefit extensions on the rise in structural unemployment are about equal to those for mismatch.[52] Differences between the researchers' estimates with regard to unemployment benefits likely reflects variations in how they operationalized the explanatory variable. Daly, Hobijn, and Valletta estimated that the temporarily authorized federal Emergency Unemployment Compensation (EUC) program accounted for 0.8 percentage points of the increase in structural unemployment from 2007 to 2010. Valletta and Kuang initially estimated a 0.4 percentage point increase in structural unemployment due to unemployment benefit extensions,[53] but after updating the data to include all of 2009 and the first half of 2010, the researchers found the effect of the EUC program to be twice as large (0.8 percentage points). Still others put the contribution of unemployment benefit extensions to increased unemployment at 0.3 percentage points,[54] 0.7-0.8 percentage points,[55] and at somewhat over 1 percentage point.[56]

Several analysts have speculated about whether the recent increase in structural unemployment will persist, thereby keeping the U.S. unemployment rate high for many years to come as occurred in some European countries from the 1980s into the 1990s.[57] Elsby, Hobijn, and Sahin stated that, despite the sharp decline in the U.S. job-finding rate, it remains well above the job-finding rates of many European countries that experienced a prolonged period of elevated structural unemployment starting in the 1980s.[58] While noting that their analysis does not suggest how long the 1.0-1.75 percentage point increase in structural unemployment due to mismatch will last, Batini, Celasun, Dowling et al. mentioned a distinctive feature of the U.S. economy—flexibility[59]—which may allow the United States to avoid stubbornly high unemployment rates for years to come.[60] Daly, Hobijn, and Valletta concluded that little of their 1.25 percentage point increase in structural unemployment is likely to persist "as labor market conditions improve [in the United States] and the extended UI provisions are allowed to expire."[61]

Taking into account changes over time in unemployment benefit programs and product market regulations, Guichard and Rusticelli estimated substantial differences in the vulnerability to structural unemployment increases among Organisation for Economic Cooperation and Development (OECD) nations.[62] Regardless of the unemployment effect of the financial crisis in the 28 OECD economies included in their 2010 study, Guichard and Rusticelli estimated that the United States may be less vulnerable than 20 nations to an increase in structural unemployment over the 2007-2012 period. Of the 10 OECD countries that experienced the largest unemployment impact from the recent financial crisis, they estimated that the United States was among the nations least vulnerable to an increase in structural unemployment.

End Notes

[1] See, for example, James Ledbetter, "Strucs vs. Cycs: The Two Gangs of Economists Warring Over the Causes of High Unemployment," *Slate*, August 24, 2010; and Prajakta Bhide, "The Fed Debates: Is Unemployment Structural or Cyclical?," *Forbes*, October 21, 2010.

[2] For additional information, see CRS Report R41578, *Unemployment: Issues in the 113th Congress*, by Jane G. Gravelle, Thomas L. Hungerford, and Linda Levine.

[3] For additional information, see CRS Report R40182, *Funding for Workforce Development in the American Recovery and Reinvestment Act (ARRA) of 2009*, by David H. Bradley and Ann Lordeman.

[4] Trend or potential economic (output) growth is dependent on the supply of labor and on productivity growth. For additional information, see CRS Report R42063, *Economic Growth and the Unemployment Rate*, by Linda Levine.

[5] Testimony of Till von Wachter, associate professor of Economics, Columbia University, in U.S. Congress, Senate Budget Committee, *Challenges for the U.S. Economic Recovery*, 112th Cong., 1st sess., February 3, 2011.

[6] Rob Valletta and Katherine Kuang, "Is Structural Unemployment on the Rise?," *FRBSF Economic Letter*, No. 2010- 34, November 8, 2010, p. 3. (Hereinafter cited as Valletta and Kuang, *Is Structural Unemployment on the Rise?*.)

[7] Calculated by CRS from the U.S. Bureau of Labor Statistics' (BLS) Current Employment Statistics (CES) program. National data from the CES program are available at http://stats.bls.gov/ces/.

[8] Valletta and Kuang, *Is Structural Unemployment on the Rise?*, p.3.

[9] J. Bradford DeLong, "Is Today's Unemployment Structural?," *The Economists' Voice*, September 2010, http://www.bepress.com/ev.

[10] BLS, Local Area Unemployment Statistics (LAUS) program. LAUS data are available at http://stats.bls.gov/lau/.

[11] CRS calculations from state-by-state employment data available through BLS's Current Employment Statistics program at http://stats.bls.gov/sae/.

[12] See, for example, Regis Barnichon and Andrew Figura, *What Drives Matching Efficiency? A Tale of Composition and Dispersion*, Federal Reserve Board, Finance and Economics Discussion Series, No. 2011-10, January 9, 2011; Henry S. Farber, "Unemployment in the Great Recession: Did the Housing Market Crisis Prevent the Unemployed from Moving to Take Jobs?," *American Economics Review*, vol. 102, no. 3 (May 2012); Alicia Sasser Modestino and Julia Dennett, *Are American Homeowners Locked into Their Houses? The Impact of Housing Market Conditions on State-to-State Migration*, Federal Reserve Bank of Boston, Working Paper no. 12-1, February 8, 2012; and Sam Schulhofer-Wohl, *Negative Equity Does Not Reduce Homeowners' Mobility*, National Bureau of Economic Research, Working Paper no. 16701, January 2011.

[13] Raven Molloy, Christopher L. Smith, and Abigail Wozniak, "Internal Migration in the United States," *Journal of Economic Perspectives*, vol. 25, no. 3 (Summer 2011), pp. 173-196.

[14] Greg Kaplan and Sam Schulhofer-Wohl, *Interstate Migration Has Fallen Less Than You Think: Consequences of Hot Deck Imputation in the Current Population Survey*, Federal Reserve Bank of Minneapolis Working Paper 681, November 2010.

[15] Daniel Aaronson and Jonathan Davis, "How Much Has House Lock Affected Labor Mobility and the Unemployment Rate?," *Chicago Fed Letter*, no. 290, September 2011.

[16] The authors used BLS's definition of displaced workers, namely, those aged 20 and older who lost their jobs after being on their employers' payrolls for at least three years prior to displacement.

[17] John Schmitt and Kris Warner, *Deconstructing Structural Unemployment*, Center for Economic and Policy Research, May 24, 2011.

[18] Robert G. Valletta, *House Lock and Structural Unemployment*, Federal Reserve Bank of San Francisco Working Paper no. 2012-25, revised November 2012.

[19] Fatih Karahan and Serena Rhee, *Geographical Reallocation and Unemployment during the Great Recession: the Role of the Housing Bust*, University of Pennsylvania, 2011, available at http://economics.sas.upenn.edu/~karahan/ JMP_Karahan.pdf.

[20] BLS defines a part-time work schedule as less than 35 hours a week.

[21] CRS calculations from Current Population Survey (CPS) data available at http://stats.bls.gov/cps/.

[22] Arjun Jayadev and Mike Konczal, *The Stagnating Labor Market*, The Roosevelt Institute, September 19, 2010, p. 8.

[23] BLS, Job Openings and Labor Turnover Survey (JOLTS) data are available at http://stats.bls.gov/jlt/.

[24] Infrastructure spending included in the American Recovery and Reinvestment Act of 2009 may have given a boost to hiring in the heavy and civil engineering component of the construction industry (i.e., establishments whose primary activity is the construction of entire engineering projects, such as highways, and specialty trade contractors whose primary activity is the production of a specific component for such projects). The law's provisions to encourage energy conservation among homeowners also may have contributed to increased labor demand in 2010 in the specialty trade contractors component of the construction industry (e.g., firms that install prefabricated thermal-pane window units and energy-efficient heating/air-conditioning units).

[25] The hiring rate of the federal government surpassed its pre-recession level in part because the Census Bureau hired temporary workers to help conduct the 2010 decennial census. For additional information, see BLS, *Census 2010 Temporary Workers and Intermittent Workers and Federal Government Employment,* available at http://stats.bls.gov/ ces/cescensusworkers.pdf; and *Impact of 2010 Census Operations on Jobs and Economic Growth*, available at http://www.esa.doc.gov/sites/default/files/reports/documents/economic growth.pdf.

[26] For additional information, see CRS Report RL32292, *Offshoring (or Offshore Outsourcing) and Job Loss Among U.S. Workers*, by Linda Levine.

[27] The distribution of employment by occupation within industries is from BLS's Occupational Employment Survey, which is available at http://stats.bls.gov/oes/.

[28] The West is composed of Alaska, Arizona, California, Colorado, Hawaii, Idaho, Montana, Nevada, New Mexico, Oregon, Utah, Washington, and Wyoming. The South is composed of Alabama, Arkansas, Delaware, District of Columbia, Florida, Georgia, Kentucky,

Louisiana, Maryland, Mississippi, North Carolina, Oklahoma, South Carolina, Tennessee, Texas, Virginia, and West Virginia.

[29] The Midwest is composed of Illinois, Indiana, Iowa, Kansas, Michigan, Minnesota, Missouri, Nebraska, North Dakota, Ohio, South Dakota, and Wisconsin.

[30] The Northeast is composed of Connecticut, Maine, Massachusetts, New Hampshire, New Jersey, New York, Pennsylvania, Rhode Island, and Vermont.

[31] CRS calculations from CPS and JOLTS data.

[32] In late 2012, there were about three jobless workers per opening.

[33] The CPS data on unemployment by industry cover persons previously employed in a given industry, which suggests that by-and-large they possessed the skills needed to qualify for the jobs they lost or left. The CPS data on unemployment discussed in the initial paragraph of this section cover all unemployed persons, that is, new entrants and reentrants to the labor force as well as persons who lost or left their jobs.

[34] Aysegul Sahin, Joseph Song, Giorgio Topa and Giovanni L. Violante, *Mismatch Unemployment*, September 2012, p. 20. It is a revised version of *Mismatch Unemployment,* National Bureau of Economic Research, Working Paper no. 18265, August 2012. (Hereinafter referred to as Sahin et al., *Mismatch Unemployment.*)

[35] See for example John Silvia and Anika Khan, "Our Two Cents on Structural Unemployment," *ABA Banking Journal*, November 2010.

[36] Kathryn J. Byun ("The U.S. Housing Bubble and Bust: Impacts on Employment," *Monthly Labor Review*, December 2010) estimated that bubble-related demand accounted for between 1.2 million and 1.7 million residential-constructionrelated jobs in 2005 at the housing bubble's peak.

[37] For additional information, see CRS Report RS22915, *Temporary Extension of Unemployment Benefits: Emergency Unemployment Compensation (EUC08)*, by Katelin P. Isaacs and Julie M. Whittaker.

[38] Testimony of Lawrence F. Katz, Harvard University, on "Long-Term Unemployment in the Great Recession," in U.S. Congress, Joint Economic Committee, *Long-Term Unemployment: Causes, Consequences and Solutions*, 111th Cong., 2nd sess., April 29, 2010.

[39] Calculated by CRS from CPS data.

[40] There was also a brief recession in 1980.

[41] Some have speculated that other displaced workers, such as those formerly employed in the finance, insurance and real estate industries, may more easily find new jobs because their skills are more readily transferable to other industries than those of construction and manufacturing workers. See for example Ellen R. Rissman, "Employment Growth: Cyclical Movements or Structural Change?," *Federal Reserve Bank of Chicago Economic Perspectives*, 4th quarter 2009, pp. 40-57.

[42] After the 1981-1982 recession, the long-term unemployed's share of total unemployment grew to 23.9%. Their share next peaked in 2003, at 22.1%, during the recovery from the 2001 recession.

[43] For additional information, see CRS Report R41179, *Long-Term Unemployment and Recessions*, by Gerald Mayer and Linda Levine.

[44] Robert Shimer, "The Probability of Finding a Job," *American Economic Review*, vol. 98, no. 2 (May 2008), pp. 268- 273.

[45] Catherine Rampell, *Will Today's Unemployed Become Tomorrow's Unemployable?*, December 2, 2010, available at http://economix.blogs.nytimes.com.

[46] Edward P. Lazear and James R. Spletzer, *The United States Labor Market: Status Quo or A New Normal?*, Paper presented at the Jackson Hole symposium, July 22, 2012, p. 32.

[47] Mark deWolf and Katherine Klemmer, "Job Openings, Hires, and Separations Fall During the Recession," *Monthly Labor Review*, May 2010, pp. 36-44.

[48] Regis Barnichon et al., "Which Industries are Shifting the Beveridge Curve?," *Monthly Labor Review*, June 2012.

[49] Mary Daly, Bart Hobijn, and Aysegul Sahin, et al.,"A Search and Matching Approach to Labor Markets: Did the Natural Rate of Unemployment Rise?," *Journal of Economic Perspectives*, vol. 26, no. 3 (summer 2012), p. 20.

[50] Sahin et al., *Mismatch Unemployment.*

[51] Benedikt Herz and Thijs van Rens, *Structural Unemployment*, Barcelona Graduate School of Economics, Working Paper no. 568, July 2011, available at http://www.crei.cat/~vanrens /SU/HvR_SU_201107.pdf.

[52] The increase in the duration of benefit eligibility to a 99-week maximum may have raised the unemployment rate above what it otherwise would have been by either reducing the number of long-term unemployed exiting the labor force or by reducing their intensity of job search and thereby decreasing the likelihood of reemployment, or both. For information on the relationship between unemployment duration and benefit receipt, see CRS Report R41676, *The Effect of Unemployment Insurance on the Economy and the Labor Market*, by Thomas L. Hungerford.

[53] Robert G. Valletta and Katherine Kuang, *Extended Unemployment and UI Benefits*, FRBSF Economic Letter, No. 2010-12, April 19, 2010.

[54] Jesse Rothstein, *Unemployment Insurance and Job Search in the Great Recession*, National Bureau of Economic Research, Working Paper no. 17534, October 2011.

[55] Daniel Aaronson, Bhashkar Mazumder, and Shani Schechter, "What is Behind the Rise in Long-Term Unemployment?," *Federal Reserve Bank of Chicago Economic Perspectives*, 2nd quarter 2010; and Bhashkar Mazumder, "How Did Unemployment Insurance Extensions Affect the Unemployment Rate in 2008-10?," *Chicago Fed Letter*, No. 285, April 2011.

[56] Shigeru Fujita, *Effects of Extended Unemployment Insurance Benefits: Evidence from the Monthly CPS*, Federal Reserve Bank of Philadelphia, Working Paper no. 10-35/R, January 2011; Steven D. Mullins, "The Unemployment Impact of the 2008 Extension of Unemployment Insurance: As High as Robert Barro Suggested?," *Economic Journal Watch*, vol. 9, no. 1, January 2012; and Makoto Nakajima, *A Quantitative Analysis of Unemployment Benefit Extension,*, Federal Reserve Bank of Philadelphia, Working Paper no. 11-8, February 8, 2011.

[57] For a discussion of institutional and other factors estimated to have led to inter-country differences in structural unemployment, see *Structural Unemployment in Western Europe*, ed. Martin Werding (Cambridge, MA: MIT Press, 2006).

[58] Michael W. Elsby, Bart Hobijn, and Aysegul Sahin, *The Labor Market in the Great Recession*, National Bureau of Economic Research, Working Paper no. 15979, May 2010. For the Brookings Panel on Economic Activity in September 2011, they along with Robert G. Valletta prepared *The Labor Market in the Great Recession: An Update,* dated October 2011, which was released by the Tinbergen Institute as Discussion Paper 2011-173/3.

[59] Structural unemployment rates vary across countries depending in part on differences in their labor market institutions or settings. The U.S. labor market is considered to be less rigid (more flexible) than that of many European countries partly because it's much lower unionization rate allows wages to adjust more quickly to economic shocks. Similarly, the relatively less generous unemployment insurance programs and lower public spending on active labor market programs (e.g., retraining) in the United States create smaller disincentives to job search among U.S. compared with European workers. See, for example,

Sven Jari Stehn, "Only a Modest Rise in Structural Unemployment So Far," *US Economics Analyst Issue No.: 10/34*, Goldman Sachs Global ECS US Research, August 27, 2010.

[60] Nicoletta Batini et al., *United States: Selected Issues Paper*, International Monetary Fund, Country Report No. 10/248, Washington, DC, July 2010, available at http://www.imf.org/external/pubs/ft/scr/2010/cr10248.pdf.

[61] Mary Daly, Bart Hobijn, and Rob Valletta, *The Recent Evolution of the Natural Rate of Unemployment*, FRBSF, Working Paper no. 2011-05, January 2011, p. 21.

[62] Stephanie Guichard and Elena Rusticelli, *Assessing the Impact of the Financial Crisis on Structural Unemployment in OECD Countries*, OECD, Economic Department Working Paper no. 767, Paris, France, October 14, 2010.

In: Labor Market Recovery ...
Editor: Kyla C. Sims

ISBN: 978-1-63117-890-0
© 2014 Nova Science Publishers, Inc.

Chapter 3

ECONOMIC GROWTH AND THE UNEMPLOYMENT RATE*

Linda Levine

SUMMARY

A persistently high unemployment rate is of concern to Congress for a variety of reasons, including its negative consequences for the economic well-being of individuals and its impact on the federal budget. The unemployment rate was 9.5% when the economy emerged from the 11th postwar recession in June 2009. It climbed further to peak at 10.0% in October 2009. The rate has slowly declined since then. Although it dropped below 8% in the fourth quarter of 2012, the unemployment rate remains high by historical standards.

After most postwar recessions, it took at least eight months for the unemployment rate to fall by one full percentage point. The slowest decline occurred following the 2001 recession's end, when the unemployment rate was a comparatively low 5.5%. About 31/2 years elapsed before the rate fell just one-half of one percentage point. In contrast, the recovery from the severe 1981-1982 recession began with the highest unemployment rate of the postwar period (10.8%). In that instance, it took only eight months for the rate to fall over one percentage point. Some hoped the unemployment rate would fall as quickly after the

* This is an edited, reformatted and augmented version of a Congressional Research Service publication, CRS Report for Congress R42063, prepared for Members and Committees of Congress, from www.crs.gov, dated January 7, 2013.

2007-2009 recession, but the speed of improvement has been more typical of the so-called jobless recoveries from the 2001 and 1990- 1991 recessions.

What appears to matter for a reduction in the unemployment rate is the size of the output gap, that is, the rate of actual output (economic) growth compared with the rate of potential output growth. Potential output is a measure of the economy's capacity to produce goods and services when resources (e.g., labor) are fully utilized. The growth rate of potential output is a function of the growth rates of potential productivity and the labor supply when the economy is at full employment. If potential output growth is about 2.5% annually at full employment, then the growth rate in real gross domestic product (GDP) would have to be greater to yield a falling unemployment rate. How much greater will determine the speed of improvement in the unemployment rate, according to a rule of thumb known as Okun's law.

In its August 2012 economic forecast, the Congressional Budget Office (CBO) estimates that the annual average growth rate of real GDP will gradually approach the growth rate of potential output over the 2012-2022 projection period. As a result of this slow narrowing of the output gap, the unemployment rate is forecast to 5.9% by 2017.

INTRODUCTION

Despite the resumption of economic (output) growth in June 2009, the unemployment rate remains at an historically high level more than three years into the recovery from the 11th recession of the postwar period. Not until the fourth quarter of 2012 did the unemployment rate drop below 8%, its lowest level since January 2009.

The persistently high unemployment rate is a cause of concern to Congress for a variety of reasons. Among them are the high rate's deleterious impact on individuals' economic well-being and the budget deficit due to lower revenue and higher expenditures. The slow rebound of the labor market has renewed calls in some quarters for measures to stimulate the economy beyond those Congress has previously enacted.[1]

From a public policy perspective, the main driver of the unemployment rate is the pace of economic growth. This report first examines the long-run relationship between the two economic variables and then narrows its focus to the periods of recovery from the postwar recessions.

THE RELATIONSHIP BETWEEN GROWTH AND UNEMPLOYMENT

In the short run, the relationship between economic growth and the unemployment rate may be a loose one. It is not unusual for the unemployment rate to show sustained decline some time after other broad measures of economic activity have turned positive. Hence, it is commonly referred to as a lagging economic indicator. One reason that unemployment may not fall appreciably when economic growth first picks up after a recession's end is that some firms may have underutilized employees on their payrolls because laying off workers when product demand declines and rehiring them when product demand improves has costs. As a result, employers may initially be able to increase output to meet rising demand at the outset of a recovery without hiring additional workers by raising the productivity of their current employees. This temporarily boosts labor productivity growth above its trend (long-run) rate.

Once the labor on hand is fully utilized, output can grow no faster than the rate of productivity growth until firms begin adding workers. As an economic expansion progresses, output growth will be determined by the combined rates of growth in the labor supply and labor productivity. As long as growth in real gross domestic product (GDP) exceeds growth in labor productivity, employment will rise. If employment growth is more rapid than labor force growth, the unemployment rate will fall.

Over an extended period of time, there is a negative relationship between changes in the rates of real GDP growth and unemployment. This long-run relationship between the two economic variables was most famously pointed out in the early 1960s by economist Arthur Okun. "Okun's law" has been included in a list of "core ideas" that are widely accepted in the economics profession.[2] Okun's law, which economists have expanded upon since it was first articulated, states that real GDP growth about equal to the rate of potential output growth usually is required to maintain a stable unemployment rate.[3]

Thus, the key to the long-run relationship between changes in the rates of GDP growth and unemployment is the rate of growth in potential output. Potential output is an unobservable measure of the capacity of the economy to produce goods and services when available resources, such as labor and capital, are fully utilized. The rate of growth of potential output is a function of the rate of growth in potential productivity and the labor supply when the economy is at full employment.[4] When the unemployment rate is high, as it is now, then actual GDP falls short of potential GDP. This is referred to as the output gap.

In the absence of productivity growth, as long as each new addition to the labor force is employed, growth in output will equal growth in the labor supply. If the rate of GDP growth falls below the rate of labor force growth, there will not be enough new jobs created to accommodate all new job seekers. As a result, the proportion of the labor force that is employed will fall. Put differently, the unemployment rate will rise. If the rate of output growth exceeds the rate of labor force growth, some of the new jobs created by employers to satisfy the rising demand for their goods and services will be filled by drawing from the pool of unemployed workers. In other words, the unemployment rate will fall.[5]

If GDP growth equals labor force growth in the presence of productivity growth, more people will be entering the labor force than are needed to produce a given amount of goods and services. The share of the labor force that is employed will fall. Expressed differently, the unemployment rate will rise. Only as long as GDP growth exceeds the combined growth rates of the labor force and productivity (potential output) will the unemployment rate fall in the long run.

Knowing what that rate of GDP growth is might be useful to policymakers interested in undertaking stimulus policies to bring down the unemployment rate. But as just stated, the rate of output growth necessary to lower the unemployment rate requires knowledge of the rates of labor force and productivity growth. Both have changed over time.

Between 1950 and 2000, the civilian labor force grew at an average annual rate of 1.6%.[6] The growth rate has slowed since then and is expected to continue doing so partly as a result of the aging of the baby-boom generation. Between 2000 and 2010, the annual rate of labor force growth fell to 0.8%. It is projected to fall further, to 0.7% per year on average, between 2010 and 2020.[7]

Predicting productivity growth is more difficult than predicting labor force growth. Economists had, until recently, identified three time periods that correspond with three different trend rates of growth in productivity.[8] Between 1947 and 1973, output per hour of labor in the private nonfarm business sector grew at an annual rate of 2.8%. Between 1973 and 1995, productivity slowed to an annual average rate of 1.4%. Between 1995 and 2005, it accelerated to 2.9% per year. Since then (2005-2011), the rate of productivity growth has slowed to 1.6% annually.[9]

If recent trends in labor force and productivity growth continue, real GDP growth above about 2.5% will be needed to push down the unemployment rate from its currently elevated level. "More specifically, according to currently accepted versions of Okun's law, to achieve a 1 percentage point decline in the unemployment rate in the course of a year, real GDP must grow approximately 2 percentage points faster than the rate of growth of potential GDP over that period."[10]

THE UNEMPLOYMENT RATE DURING POSTWAR RECOVERIES

As previously discussed, it is not unusual for some time to elapse between the start of an economic recovery and the start of a declining unemployment rate. Suppose that two successive monthly declines are taken as the beginning of a meaningful downward trend in the unemployment rate. *Table 1* shows how long it has taken following the end of each of the 11 economic contractions for that trend to begin.

Table 1. Months Between the Start of a Recovery and Two Successive Declines in the Unemployment Rate

Date of Start of Recovery	Months After Recovery's Start and Two Successive Declines in Unemployment Rate
October 1949	4
May 1954	6
April 1958	5
February 1961	9
November 1970	11
March 1975	4
July 1980	2
November 1982	5
March 1991	17
November 2001	21
June 2009	12

Source: Calculated by CRS based on business cycle troughs from the National Bureau of Economic Research and unemployment rates from the U.S. Bureau of Labor Statistics.

At one extreme, it was well over a year following the start of the economy's rebound from the 1990-1991 and 2001 recessions before the unemployment rate began to steadily decline. This contributed to the two periods being labeled jobless recoveries.

At the other extreme, the unemployment rate began trending downward at five or fewer months after the end of five earlier recessions. The current recovery lies within but closer to the high-end of this range. As the unemployment rate experienced two successive monthly declines 12 months after the start of the recovery from the 2007-2009 recession, it too was dubbed a jobless recovery.

Not only has the length of time for the unemployment rate to begin falling varied by recovery, but its pace of decline also has varied. After eight of the eleven postwar recessions, it took at least eight months for the unemployment rate to fall by one full percentage point.[11] The slowest decline occurred after the recession that ended in November 2001 when the unemployment rate stood at 5.5%, the lowest unemployment rate recorded at the start of an expansion. About 31/2 years elapsed before the unemployment rate fell one-half of a percentage point. In contrast, the expansion that followed the July 1981-November 1982 downturn began with the highest unemployment rate of the postwar period (10.8%). In that case, it took only eight months for the unemployment rate to fall more than one percentage point (to a still high 9.4%).

A debate recently broke out over the applicability of Okun's law to changes in economic growth and the unemployment rate.[12] Following a period of growth rates early in the recovery high enough (above 3.5%) to have produced a downward trend in the unemployment rate, the unemployment rate stalled at about 9.0% in the first three quarters of 2011. This resulted from slow annual growth in real GDP of 0.1% in the first quarter, 2.5% in the second quarter, and 1.3% in the third quarter of 2011.[13] Output growth accelerated at an annual rate of 4.1% in the fourth quarter of 2011, and the unemployment rate resumed its downward trend—dropping to 8.5% in December 2011.

But as noted by the chairman of the Federal Reserve Board at a March 2012 conference of economists,

> the decline in the unemployment rate over the course of 2011 was greater than would seem consistent with GDP growth over that period. Indeed, with last year's real GDP growth below 2 percent, less than what most economists would estimate to be the U.S. economy's potential rate

of growth, one might have expected little change in the unemployment rate last year or even a slight increase.[14]

Bernanke suggested that this temporary disconnect may have compensated for an earlier deviation from Okun's law. In 2009, workers were laid off and the unemployment rate rose beyond the level commensurate with the contraction in economic growth.

When McCarthy, Potter, and Ng at the New York Federal Reserve Bank examined long recovery periods after the trough of the three recessions before the 2007-2009 recession,[15] they estimated that Okun's law underpredicted the actual decline in the unemployment rate.[16] Others similarly estimated periods of instability in the relationship between the rates of economic growth and unemployment.[17]

Some of the variation may be due to the stage of the business cycle, with the rule of thumb perhaps holding up better during recessions than recoveries.[18] Based on their analysis, Owyang and Sekhposyan suggest "that back-of-the-envelope calculations used to relate changes in the unemployment rate to changes in output growth or the output gap should not be taken too seriously but rather as an approximation to be taken with a grain of salt."[19]

In contrast, Ball et al estimated that, as posited by Okun, increases and decreases in output have the same effect on unemployment. In other words, the rule-of-thumb applies equally well to recoveries and recessions. They also demonstrated that Okun's law did not break down during the recent jobless recoveries.

Between 2009 and 2011, for example, Ball et al estimated that the relationship between output and unemployment gaps approximated the relationship predicted by Okun. The difference between the recoveries from the 1990-1991, 2001, and 2007-2009 recessions and recoveries from earlier recessions appears to be that large output gaps (i.e., slow economic growth relative to trend) persisted well into the three jobless (high-unemployment) recoveries.

The researchers conclude by stating that "it is rare to call a macroeconomic relationship a 'law.' Yet we believe that Okun's Law has earned its name.

It is not as universal as the law of gravity ... , but it is strong and stable by the standards of macroeconomics. Reports of deviations from the Law are often exaggerated."[20]

The Outlook for the Unemployment Rate in the Next Few Years

According to estimates by economist Robert J. Gordon, potential output has grown at an average annual rate of 3.4% since 1875.[21] Gordon doubts, however, that growth in potential GDP will be that rapid over the next 20 years as gains from information technology investments have been diminishing. His assumption of slower productivity growth along with the previously discussed expected declines in labor force growth led him to project a 2.4% rate of growth in potential output over the next 20 years. If that view is correct, then real economic growth in excess of 2.4% would be likely to yield a declining rate of unemployment.

Economists Susanto Basu and John G. Fernald also examined the current outlook for growth in potential output.[22] They point out that household net worth declined significantly during the 2007-2009 recession. That drop in wealth, they argue, will make it more difficult for workers to afford leisure time (e.g., retirement). Consequently, the supply of labor may be larger in the near term than it might otherwise have been. This would tend to temporarily raise growth in potential output. At the same time, Basu and Fernald expect that disruptions in financial markets will tend to constrain growth in potential output over the near term because of higher risks associated with investment spending. These offsetting factors mainly serve to emphasize how uncertain estimates of growth in potential output can be.

Weidner and Williams examined the relationship between real economic growth and the strength of past recoveries. The economists estimate that potential output growth was comparatively rapid during the initial expansions of the 1960s through 1980s (at 3.6%). In contrast, potential output was much more moderate (2.5%) during the first two years of recovery from the 1990-1991 and 2001 recessions. They estimate potential GDP growth at the outset of the recovery from the Great Recession[23] was a more sluggish 2.1% due to the slow rate of labor force growth.[24] If they are correct, real economic growth greater than 2.1% would likely produce a falling unemployment rate.

The Congressional Budget Office (CBO) regularly publishes projections of growth in potential output. In its August 2012 economic outlook, CBO forecast that potential output of the overall economy will grow at an average annual rate of 2.2% between 2012 and 2022.[25] In contrast, the agency estimated a considerably higher average annual growth rate of potential GDP between 1950 and 2011 (3.3%). The lower projection of potential output growth going forward chiefly reflects CBO's projection of greatly reduced potential labor force growth (from 1.5% between 1950 and 2011 to 0.5% between 2012 and 2022) mostly due to increasing retirements among workers of the baby-boom generation.

CBO also projected in August 2012 that the annual average growth rate of real GDP will stay below the growth rate of potential output until 2018. The annual average rate of unemployment is therefore estimated to remain above 8.0% through 2014, and then fall to 5.9% by 2017 as the output gap progressively narrows.

End Notes

[1] For additional information, see CRS Report R41578, Unemployment: Issues in the 113th Congress, by Jane G. Gravelle, Thomas L. Hungerford, and Linda Levine.

[2] Alan Blinder, "Is There A Core of Practical Macroeconomics That We Should All Believe?," American Economic Review, vol. 87, no. 2, May 1997.

[3] Knotek updated Okun's analysis, which covered the 1948-1960 period, to 2007 and came to much the same conclusion. Specifically, real output growth of about 4.0% is consistent with a stable unemployment rate. This means that in the long run faster output growth usually coincided with a decreasing unemployment rate, whereas output growth below 4% usually coincided with an increasing unemployment rate. See Edward S. Knotek, "How Useful is Okun's Law?," Federal Reserve Bank of Kansas City, Economic Review, fourth quarter 2007. (Hereinafter referred to as Knotek, How Useful is Okun's Law.)

[4] Full employment is said to be achieved when the unemployment rate is at a level consistent with a stable (non-accelerating) inflation rate.

[5] Once unemployment reaches relatively low levels, the increased demand for labor is more likely to be satisfied by rising wages than by higher levels of employment. There may be a risk of accelerating inflation as a result. The Congressional Budget Office estimated that the rate close to which that becomes a risk (which is referred to as the nonaccelerating inflation rate of unemployment or NAIRU) may be about 5%. (See Robert Arnold, Reestimating the Phillips Curve and the NAIRU, CBO, Working Paper 2008-06, August 2008.) At the current level of the unemployment rate, the risk of accelerating wages and inflation seems low. It also seems low at even higher estimates of NAIRU, which ranged from 6.2% to 8.2% for the first quarter of 2011 according to estimates by Weidner and Williams (Update of "How Big is the Output Gap?," Federal Reserve Bank of San Francisco, July 7, 2011).

[6] Mitra Toossi, "A Century of Change: the U.S. Labor Force, 1950-2050," Monthly Labor Review, May 2002.

[7] Mitra Toossi, "Labor Force Projections to 2020: A More Slowly Growing Workforce," January 2012.

[8] See for example Michael Chernousov, Susan E. Fleck, and John Glaser, "Productivity Trends in Business Cycles," Monthly Labor Review, June 2009; and J. Bradford DeLong, "Productivity Growth in the 2000s," National Bureau of Economic Research, Macroeconomics Annual, vol. 17 (2000).

[9] Calculated by CRS from BLS productivity data, available at http://www.bls.gov.

[10] Chairman Ben S. Bernanke at the National Association for Business Economics annual conference, Washington, DC, March 26, 2012, available at http://www.federalreserve.gov/newsevents/speech/bernanke20120326a.htm. (Hereinafter referred to as Bernanke, NABE conference address.)

[11] They are the recoveries from the 1960-1961, 1969-1970, 1973-1975, 1980, 1981-1982, 1990-1991, 2001, and 2007-2009 recessions.

[12] See for example Nin-Hai Tseng, "Jobless Numbers Defy Economic Theory," CNNMoney, March 15, 2012, available at http://finance.fortune.cnn.com/2012/03/16/okuns-law/.

[13] U.S. Bureau of Economic Analysis, National Income and Product Accounts data, available at http://www.bea.gov.

[14] Bernanke, NABE conference address.

[15] Years two through five from the end of the 1981-1982, 1990-1991, and 2001 recessions.

[16] Jonathan McCarthy, Simon Potter, and Ging Cee Ng, "Okun's Law and Long Expansions," Federal Reserve Bank of New York, March 27, 2012.

[17] See for example Brent Meyer and Murat Tasci, "An Unstable Okun's Law, Not the Best Rule of Thumb," Federal Reserve Bank of Cleveland, Economic Trends, June 7, 2012.

[18] Knotek, How Useful Is Okun's Law and Emily Burgen, Brent Meyer and Murat Tasci, "An Elusive Relation Between Unemployment and GDP Growth: Okun's Law, Federal Reserve Bank of Cleveland, Economic Trends, April 5, 2012.

[19] Michael T. Owyang and Tatevik Sekhposyan, "Okun's Law over the Business Cycle: Was the Great Recession All That Different?", Federal Reserve Bank of St. Louis REVIEW, September/October 2012, p.417.

[20] Laurence Ball, Daniel Leigh, and Prakash Loungani, Okun's Law: Fit at 50?, paper presented at the 13th Jacques Polak Annual Research Conference hosted by the International Monetary Fund, Washington, DC, November 8-9, 2012, p. 22.

[21] Robert J. Gordon, "The Slowest Potential Output Growth in U.S. History: Measurement and Interpretation," presented at the Center for the Study of Innovation and Productivity at the Federal Reserve Bank of San Francisco, November 2008.

[22] Susanto Basu and John G. Fernald, What Do We Know and Not Know About Potential Output?, Federal Reserve Bank of San Francisco, Working Paper, March 2009.

[23] The 2007-2009 recession is commonly referred to as the Great Recession.

[24] Justin Weidner and John C. Williams, "The Shape of Things to Come," Federal Reserve Bank of San Francisco, Economic Letter, May 17, 2010.

[25] Congressional Budget Office, An Update of the Budget and Economic Outlook: Fiscal Years 2012 to 2022, August 2012.

In: Labor Market Recovery ...
Editor: Kyla C. Sims
ISBN: 978-1-63117-890-0
© 2014 Nova Science Publishers, Inc.

Chapter 4

THE UNEMPLOYED AND JOB OPENINGS: A DATA PRIMER*

Donald Hirasuna

SUMMARY

New information that adds to the mix of labor market indicators may be useful to Congress. The ratio of unemployed persons per job opening provides information on how many unemployed persons on average there are for every job opening. It adds to the current mix of labor market indicators such as the unemployment rate, which is a measure of the excess supply of workers. In addition, it adds to employment statistics, which measures the demand for workers that have already been met by employers. By dividing the number of unemployed persons with the number of job openings, the ratio gauges the excess supply of workers relative to the demand, where job openings serve as a measure of the unmet need for workers. The resultant statistic compares the number of persons who are actively searching for jobs to the number of available opportunities.

Four key findings arise from this analysis:

1) The ratio of unemployed persons per job opening is highly correlated with the unemployment rate between 2001 and 2012.

---

* This is an edited, reformatted and augmented version of Congressional Research Service Publication, No. R42943, dated January 31, 2013.

2) The ratio of unemployed persons per job opening rises during the recessionary periods covered in this data set. In the 2007-2009 recession, the ratio rises to very high levels, especially in the goods-producing industries (construction, manufacturing, mining and logging).
3) Although the ratio is highly correlated with changes in the unemployment rate, the ratio saw modest improvements coming out of the recent recession sooner than the reductions in the unemployment rate.
4) Even though the ratio has reduced, it remains at higher levels than prior to the 2007-2009 recession.

The analysis in this report combines two data sources:

- The *Job Openings and Labor Turnover Survey (JOLTS)*, which provide information from a survey of U.S. business establishments on the dynamic job market where job openings are created, persons are hired, and employees leave.
- The *Current Population Survey (CPS)*, which provides information on economic and demographic information from U.S. households.

INTRODUCTION

The Bureau of Labor Statistics (BLS) publishes job openings data from the Job Openings and Labor Turnover Survey (JOLTS). Data on job openings provide information on the number of workers that employers intend to hire in the near future. This information enriches knowledge of the U.S. labor market adding to current information on unemployment rates and employment.

Many labor market indicators provide information on either the supply or demand for workers. Unemployment rates provide information on the supply of persons seeking work in excess of those currently employed. Alternatively, employment provides information on the demand for workers that is already met by employers.

This report provides information on the ratio of unemployed persons per job opening, which may be useful to Congress in that it adds nuanced information to the current mix of labor market indicators. The ratio is unique in that it combines both supply and demand measures. Using unemployed persons from the Current Population Survey (CPS) and job openings from the JOLTS, the ratio divides the number of persons generally aged 16 and older who are not employed and actively looking for jobs by the number of job openings. The advantage to the statistic is that the ratio gauges the excess supply of labor relative to the unmet needs of employers. The ratio may add useful information to data on job openings or unemployment in that it takes into consideration how many persons are actively searching for work relative to the number of opportunities.

Specifically, in this report, trends in the ratio of unemployed persons per job opening are tracked from January 2001 through February 2012.[1] Comparisons are made with the unemployment rate, which has been used as a primary labor market indicator for many years. Figures and tables are provided that show the ratio in the aggregate for the United States and across industrial sectors.

Four key findings arise from this analysis:

1) The ratio of unemployed persons per job opening is highly correlated with the unemployment rate between 2001 and 2012.
2) The ratio of unemployed persons per job opening rises during the recessionary periods covered in this data set. In the 2007-2009 recession, the ratio rises to very high levels, especially in the goods-producing industries (construction, manufacturing, mining and logging).
3) Although the ratio is highly correlated with changes in the unemployment rate, the ratio saw modest improvements coming out of the recent recession sooner than the reductions in the unemployment rate.
4) Even though the ratio has reduced, it remains at higher levels than prior to the 2007-2009 recession.

UNEMPLOYMENT AND JOB OPENINGS

This section separately examines the two statistics in the ratio, unemployment and job openings. The ratio is built by placing the number of unemployed persons in the numerator and dividing by the number of job openings. Separately examining the trends in unemployment and job openings may add to understanding of policy issues related to the U.S. labor market. Comparing how these statistical indicators fluctuate through the economic cycles covered in this report may help in understanding trends in the ratio of unemployed persons per job opening.

From January 2001 through February 2012, job openings fluctuated with the economy in countercyclical movement with the number of unemployed persons. Job openings are more numerous when the economy is growing and are fewer in number when the economy is in recession. During economic expansion, business establishments begin to sell more goods and services and correspondingly hire more workers. As the economy contracts or enters a recession, businesses need fewer workers and businesses may more likely freeze their job vacancies, close the opportunity or lay off workers. Unemployment rates rise during recessions as more persons are laid-off, and other persons looking for a job are unable to find work. Not all businesses hire and not all persons are employed during economic expansion, but the overall cyclical trend is observed at the aggregate level when summing across all employer establishments.

Figure 1 depicts the monthly number of unemployed and job openings from January 2001 through February 2012. The upper line is the total number of unemployed and the lower line is the total number of job openings. Each point in both lines represents a month, where the months are listed along the x-axis.

From the periods covered in this report, January 2001 through February 2012, the U.S. economy underwent two recessions, which are indicated by the shaded columns in **Figure 1**. The beginning and ending dates of each recession are determined by the Business Cycle Dating Committee of the National Bureau of Economic Research (NBER). The NBER declares a recession during the months when economic activity declines from its peak to its trough.[2] The NBER further defines economic expansion as the period from trough to peak. The first recession begins in March 2001and ends in November 2001, which will be referred to as the 2001 recession. The second is from December 2007 through June 2009 and is referred to as the 2007-2009 recession.

From January 2001 through February 2012, the number of unemployed persons fluctuates upward during recession and downward during most months of economic expansion. The number of unemployed persons decreases to 6.7 million in March 2007. In the following months, the total number of unemployed persons turns back upward reaching7.6 million during the first month of the 2007-2009 recession. In the months during the recession, unemployment rises more sharply reaching a high of 15.4 million persons in October 2009. Afterward, unemployment modestly decreases to 12.8 million in February 2012.

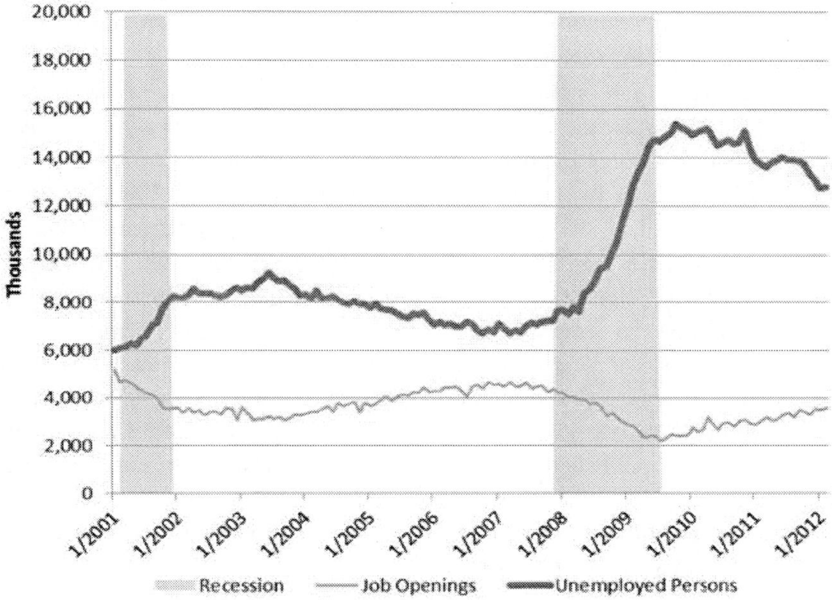

Source: Data on unemployment are from the Current Population Survey (CPS) and data on job openings are from the Job Openings and Labor Turnover Survey (JOLTS).

Notes: See Table 1 for information on unemployment and job openings data.

Figure 1. Job Openings and Unemployed Persons in the United States. Monthly Data from January 2001 Through February 2012; Data are Adjusted for Seasonality.

Job openings also fluctuate with the business cycle, but increased during most expansionary months and decreased during recession. **Figure 1** shows that in months following the 2001 recession, total job openings reaches its highest number of 4.7 million in November 2006 and again in March 2007. Afterward, job openings decrease as the economy entered the 2007-2009 recession. A low point of 2.2 million job openings is reached one month after the end of the recession in July 2009. After the recession, job openings turn back upwards and as of the end of the data on February 2012, the total number reached 3.6 million.

Job openings differ from unemployment in that job openings led unemployment in the movement away from the troughs and peaks since 2006. Job openings began to increase in July whereas unemployment rates did not reach a high until October 2009. In 2007, job openings fell from the high point of 4.7 million in March of 2007, whereas the unemployment rate did not increase until two months later in May of 2007.[3]

If changes in job openings lead changes in unemployment, it may prove useful when considering some labor market policies. Whether job openings can anticipate a change in unemployment is uncertain. Although job openings led in the movement away from the high and low points after 2006, it may be coincidence, because job openings did not lead unemployment in 2003. Job openings reached a low of 3.1 million in September 2003 and unemployed persons reached a high of 0.2 million three months earlier in June 2003. More years of information would be needed to assess whether job openings might serve as an early indicator to changes in unemployment and under what circumstances. A further consideration is that even if job openings can serve as a leading indicator, its potential in practice is hampered because preliminary estimates are not published until two months after the survey is conducted and final estimates are published one month after the preliminary estimates. This means that preliminary estimates for November and final estimates for October are not available until January.[4]

THE RATIO OF UNEMPLOYED PERSONS PER JOB OPENING: TRENDS AND COMPARISONS

This section introduces the ratio of unemployed persons per job opening and discusses trends in the ratio over time. A brief comparison with a few other commonly used labor market indicators is conducted to highlight the nuanced information added by the ratio. This section also includes some technical notes about the ratio and the data.

As a brief introduction, the ratio of unemployed persons per job opening is constructed by taking the number of unemployed persons and dividing it by the number of job openings.[5] Lower values for the ratio imply fewer unemployed persons for every job opening and possibly greater ease in finding a job. Higher values would indicate more unemployed persons searching for the same number of jobs and potentially more difficulty in finding work.

The ratio uniquely combines supply and demand measures of the labor market. The number of unemployed persons is a measure of persons looking for work, or the supply of labor in excess of those currently employed. Job openings are a measure of the demand for workers that are not currently met by employers. It can be used to consider how easy it may be to find a job given both the number of other persons looking for work and the number of available job openings. Fewer unemployed persons or more job openings may both contribute to a greater ease in finding work. [6]

This section has four findings. The first sub-section on trends in the ratio establishes three of the basic findings: First, the ratio of unemployed persons per job opening is highly correlated with the unemployment rate between 2001 and 2012. Second, the ratio of unemployed persons per job opening rises during the recessionary periods covered in this data set. In the 2007-2009 recession, the ratio rises to very high levels. Third, even though the ratio has reduced, it remains at higher levels than prior to the 2007-2009 recession. The following section discussing the ratio of unemployed persons per job opening as a unique indicator identifies a fourth finding: While the ratio is highly correlated with changes in the unemployment rate, the ratio saw modest improvements coming out of the recent recession sooner than the reductions in the unemployment rate.

Trends in the Ratio of Unemployed Persons per Job Opening: Basic Findings

Figure 2 graphs the monthly ratio of unemployed person per job opening from January 2001 through February 2012. The x-axis is in months and the y-axis on the left is the numerical value for the ratio. The figure also charts the unemployment rate, which is a commonly used labor market indicator. Values for the unemployment rate are listed on the y-axis on the right.

Figure 2 establishes three basic findings in this dataset. Sections to follow will further refine the conclusions from this section.

Finding 1

The ratio of unemployed persons per job opening is highly correlated with the unemployment rate between 2001 and 2012. **Figure 2** shows that the unemployed persons per job opening ratio and the unemployment rate fluctuate with the business cycle. Both increase within months of the recession and decrease during economic expansion. Although not perfect, the two labor market indicators have roughly corresponded with the economy.

The unemployed persons per job opening ratio rises with increases in the numerator (unemployment) or decreases in the denominator (job openings). An increase in unemployment raises the numerator suggesting more persons searching for work for the same number of jobs. Fewer job openings lower the denominator suggesting fewer opportunities for the same number of unemployed. As discussed in the previous section, job openings and unemployment follow the business cycle. The number of unemployed persons increases during periods of recession and decreases during most months of economic expansion. In contrast, job openings decrease during periods of recession and increase during most months of economic expansion.

The unemployment rate divides the number of unemployed by the number of persons in the labor force, where persons in the labor force are 16 years and older and are either employed or actively searching for work. More unemployed persons raise the numerator to the unemployment rate. Alternatively, fewer labor force participants lower the denominator, which also raises the unemployment rate.

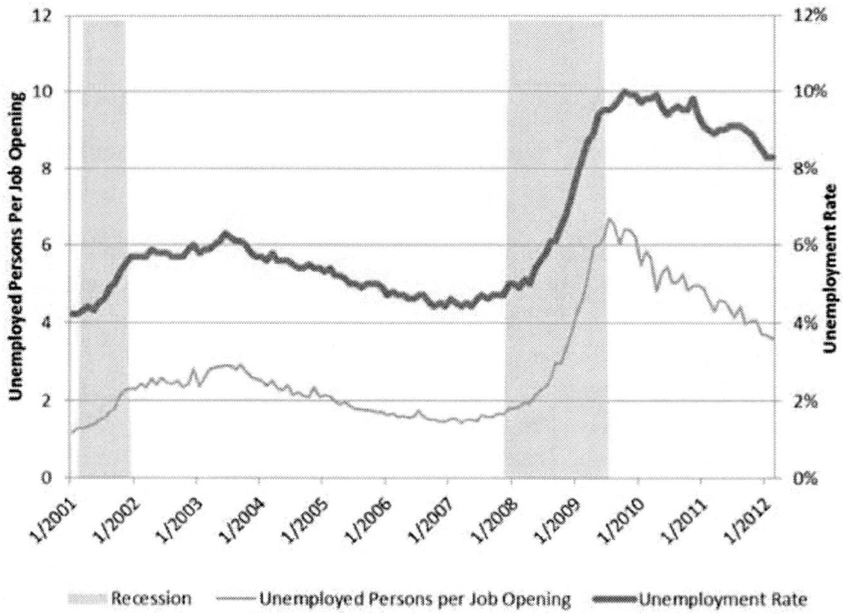

Source: Data on unemployment levels and rates are from the CPS and data on job openings are from the JOLTS.

Notes: See Table 1 for information on unemployment and job openings data.

Figure 2. Ratio of Unemployed Persons Per Job Opening and the Unemployment Rate. Monthly Data from January 2001 through February 2012, Adjusted for Seasonality.

Finding 2

The ratio of unemployed persons per job opening rises during the recessionary periods covered in this data set. In the 2007-2009 recession, the ratio rises to very high levels. **Figure 2** shows that the ratio of unemployed persons per job opening rises throughout the 2001 recession reaching its high point in September 2003. The ratio declines during most of the months of economic expansion until March 2007, 10 months before the beginning of the 2007-2009 recession. Afterward, the ratio increases from 1.4 in March of 2007 to 1.8 in December of 2007.

During the 2007-2009 recession, the ratio of unemployed persons per job opening rises to its highest level in the period covered for this report. During the first year, from December 2007 through November 2008, the ratio of unemployed persons per job opening increases from 1.8 to 3.3. From December 2008 to one-month after the end of the recession in July 2009, the ratio increases more sharply to a high of 6.7. This exceeds roughly three times the high point that occurs following the 2001 recession, which was 2.9 in September 2003.

The unemployment rate similarly fluctuates with the business cycle with higher rates during recession and lower rates during most months of economic expansion. The unemployment rate in January 2001 was 4.2%. The rate rises through the 2001 recession reaching a high of 6.3%.

As the economy expanded, **Figure 2** shows that the unemployment rate decreases to a low of 4.4% in October of 2006. Unemployment rates turn back upward again as the economy enters the 2007-2009 recession. During the recession, unemployment rates rise sharply, especially during the last year. The rate reaches a high of 10.0% in October 2009. Since then, unemployment rates have lowered to approximately 8%.

Finding 3

Even though both ratios have reduced, they remain at higher levels than prior to the 2007-2009 recession. As of February 2012, the ratio of unemployed persons per job opening is 3.6. This is higher than the 2.9 that occurred in September of 2003, which is the high point of all the monthly ratios prior to the most recent recession. As seen in the next section, even though the ratio is high, when compared with the unemployment rate and other labor market indicators, it has improved more substantially since the end of the recession.

A Unique Ratio: Differences from the Unemployment Rate and Other Labor Market Measures

This section highlights the uniqueness of the ratio by its virtue of combining both supply and demand measures. A key finding is that while the ratio is highly correlated with changes in the unemployment rate, the ratio saw modest improvements coming out of the recent recession sooner than the reductions in the unemployment rate. In addition, the correlation between the ratio and the unemployment rate has at least temporarily changed since the 2007-2009 recession, where the difference appears to arise from stagnant growth in the labor force. Finally, even though the ratio shows modest reductions, actual hires may have lagged behind job openings. This further highlights a potential issue in the labor market that jobs may currently be more difficult to find than indicated by the ratio in prior years.

The ratio of unemployed persons per job opening may serve as a useful addition to other labor market indicators. First there may be some chance that the ratio of unemployed persons per job opening may be a leading indicator to changes in the unemployment rates. The ratio of unemployed persons per job opening reached a high in July of 2009, whereas the unemployment rate reached its high four months later in October 2009. Like job openings, however, this is uncertain because the ratio did not lead the decrease in unemployment rates after the 2001 recession.

Second, **Figure 2** shows the difference between the unemployment rate and the ratio of unemployed persons per job opening is fairly constant prior to the 2007-2009 recession.[7] Afterward, the ratio of unemployed persons per job opening fell by a larger amount in comparison to the unemployment rate. The shift in the relationship seems to suggest that, at least temporarily, the same ratios of unemployed persons per job opening are associated with higher unemployment rates. A decrease in the ratio potentially indicating a greater ease in finding a job does not correspond with as large of a decrease in the unemployment rate. Whether the shift in the relationship is permanent may depend upon other labor market conditions.

The differences in the measures arise because the unemployment rate is a measure of excess supply and the ratio of unemployed persons per job opening combines measures of supply and demand. More specifically, the difference is in the denominator. Both measures have the number of unemployed in the numerator. The unemployment rate divides the number of unemployed persons by the number of persons in the labor force. The ratio of unemployed persons per job opening divides the unemployed by the number of job openings. There has been a modest recovery in job openings yet labor force participation appears to remain at lower levels. **Figure 1** shows that the number of job openings increased by 63.1% from July 2007 to February 2012 (from 2.2 to 3.6 million). By comparison, participants in the labor force increased by a smaller 0.2% during this same period (from 154.5 to 154.8 million).

When examining other labor market indicators, the ratio appears to add some nuance to a description of current labor market conditions. A variety of labor market indicators show that the 2007-2009 recession is one of the most severe recessions in the post-World War II era. Unemployment, employment, labor force participation, and hours worked all indicated a substantial deterioration in labor market conditions. Since the 2007-2009 recession, the combination of statistics suggest modest growth in employment, but stagnant growth in labor force participation. The ratio of unemployed persons per job opening suggests more marked gains in the ease at which unemployed persons might find jobs, but even though jobs may be open, establishments may not be hiring as much. From the end of the recession in June 2009 to February 2012, unemployment and the unemployment rate modestly decreased. Employment increased by a modest 2.0%. Similar to stagnant growth in labor force participation, the employment to population ratio has decreased by 1.1% from July 2009 to February 2012. The job openings rate has increased by 52.9%. However, the hires rate, the proportion of hires relative to jobs plus new hires increases by a smaller 13.8%. These statistics suggest modest reductions in unemployment, modest gains in employment, but stagnant growth in the labor force and hires falling below job opportunities.[8]

A Primer on Data and Methodology

The ratio of unemployed Persons per job opening is calculated as

$$\textit{Unemployed Persons Per Job Opening} = \frac{\textit{Number of Unemployed Persons}}{\textit{Number of Job Openings}}$$

The indicator is constructed with two datasets. Job openings is a measure of the unmet demand for workers and the data on employers' demand come from the Job Openings and Labor Turnover Survey (JOLTS), which is a survey of about 16,000 business establishments. Unemployed is a measure of the excess supply of workers and comes from the Current Population Survey, a survey of approximately 60,000 households.

To ensure consistency in the data, the BLS defines both job openings and unemployment. Among other criteria, a job opening is a specific position that is open on the last business day of the month and the establishment must be able to start the job within 30 days. In general, unemployment is defined as an individual who is at least 16 years old, is not employed during the reference week, but available for work. Usually the reference week includes the 12th day of the month.

There are several limitations to the ratio that often apply to other aggregate statistics on the labor market. For example, differences in the ratio across occupations or earnings levels are not available. A job opening in one region of the United States may be temporarily inaccessible to a person living in another region, because that person would have to relocate to take that job. See the Appendix for more information on the data and its limitations.

DIFFERENCES ACROSS INDUSTRIAL SECTORS

Sector level information on the ratio of unemployed persons per job opening might lead to a better understanding of the trends in the aggregate ratio over time. Decomposing the aggregate ratio into its industrial sector shows substantial differences in trends, especially during the height of the 2007-2009 recession. The ratio for the goods-producing sector rises significantly above the other sectors serving to further drive upward the aggregate ratio of unemployed persons per job opening.[9]

This section examines the ratio of unemployed persons per job opening for four industrial sectors: (1) goods-producing, (2) producer services, (3) consumer services, and (4) government.[10] Goods production is defined here as the production of tangible items, such as cell phones and HD-TVs. The goods-producing sector is made up of three sub-sectors, or industries. These are mining and logging, construction, and manufacturing. Services in turn are defined as the production of everything else within the private-business sector. Because services make up a significant percentage of the number of jobs (83% in February 2012), this sector is further divided in services that are purchased primarily by producers or by consumers. Examples of producer services include financial activities and information services. Consumer services include industries such as retail trade and education and health services.

Table 1. Average Monthly Number of Job Openings, Unemployed Persons and Unemployed Persons Per Job Opening by Sector and Industry for Calendar Year 2011

Sector or Industry	Number of Job Openings In Thousands	Percentage of Total Number of Job Openings	Number of Unemployed Persons In Thousands	Percentage of Total Number of Unemployed Persons	Unemployed Persons Per Job Opening
Goods-Producing	342.0	10.6%	2,807.8	24.1%	8.2
Mining and Logging	28.1	0.9%	52.0	0.4%	1.9
Construction	81.5	2.5%	1,383.3	11.9%	17.0
Manufacturing	232.4	7.2%	1,372.5	11.8%	5.9
Producer Services	933.3	29.0%	2,234.3	19.1%	2.4
Information	103.7	3.2%	222.0	1.9%	2.1
Financial Activities	205.5	6.4%	582.1	5.0%	2.8
Professional and Business Services	624.2	19.4%	1,430.2	12.3%	2.3
Consumer Services	1,605.3	49.9%	5,613.7	48.1%	3.5
Trade, Transportation, and Utilities	540.8	16.8%	2,318.2	19.9%	4.3
Education and Health Services	582.3	18.1%	1,216.8	10.4%	2.1
Leisure and Hospitality	362.3	11.3%	1,527.3	13.1%	4.2
Other Services	119.8	3.7%	551.4	4.7%	4.6
Government	335.3	10.4%	1,013.5	8.7%	3.0

Source: Data on unemployed persons are from the Current Population Survey (CPS) and data on job openings are from the Job Openings and Labor Turnover Survey (JOLTS).

Notes: The averages are calculated using monthly statistics within the calendar year that were not adjusted for seasonality. See Table 1 for information on unemployment and job openings data.

Table 1 shows the average monthly number of job openings, unemployed persons, and unemployed persons per job opening by sector and industry for 2011, where "unemployment from an industry" is the industry that the person last worked. The table helps show which industries are assigned to which sectors. Also, as shown by the numbers in the table, sectors can make up a large share of unemployed persons or job openings and still have a relatively small ratio of unemployed persons per job opening. A larger ratio of unemployed persons per job opening occurs when the sector has a larger share of unemployed persons relative to its share of job openings.[11] For example, consumer services comprise the largest share of unemployed persons (48.1) and largest share of job openings (49.9%). However, the ratio of unemployed persons per job opening is 3.5, which is lower than the 8.2 for the goods-producing sector. The higher ratio in the goods-producing sector is reflected by the fact that it has a higher percentage of unemployment (24.1%) relative to its share of job openings (10.6%). Producer services have a relatively lower share of unemployment (19.1%) relative to its job openings (29.0%) and have the lowest ratio of unemployed persons per job opening at 2.4.

What this further implies is that the ratio does not say anything about the size of the sector. A higher ratio of unemployed persons per job opening might occur in sectors with relatively few unemployed persons or job openings. To know something about the size of the sector, the actual numbers of unemployed persons and job openings are needed.

Table 1 shows the ratio of unemployed persons per job opening by sector for each month from January 2001 through February 2012. The figure highlights several consistent patterns across industrial sectors. First the ratios are consistently higher for the goods-producing sector possibly indicating increased difficulty in finding work. As shown in the figure, from January 2001 through February 2012, the ratio is consistently higher in the goods-producing sector regardless of the economic cycle.

Second, the ratio is much more variable within the goods-producing sector. By the end of the recession in June 2009, the ratio of unemployed persons per job opening rises to 22.2 for the goods-producing sector. This is in comparison to ratios of 4.7 for producer services, 4.4 for consumer services and 2.9 for the government sectors. After the recession, the ratio in the goods-producing sector fell by a larger amount than any other sector—by 14.4 unemployed persons for every job opening in the goods-producing sector, 2.2 for producer services, 1.2 for consumer services and 0.7 for government—from June 2009 to February 2012.[12]

The higher ratios in the goods-producing sector are accompanied by decreases in employment within this sector. Goods-producing employment drops from 22.0 million in December 2007 to a low of 17.7 million in February 2010, seven months after the end of the recession. The 4.3 million decreases in employment is larger than the 2.4 million decrease in producer services and 2.1 million decrease in consumer services, which occur during the same months.[13]

How much employment in the goods-producing sector relates to cyclical aspects of the economy, or how much is part of a long-term trend of decreased employment, is uncertain.[14] In February 2012, employment in the goods-producing sector was 18.2 million, a 0.5 million increase from the depth of the recession, but still lower than months preceding the recession. At the beginning of the recession in December 2007, goods-producing employment was 22.0 million and was even higher yet in January 2001 at 24.5 million. To return to the January 2001 employment levels, goods-producing employment would have to increase by 34.6% (8.3 million). In manufacturing, which is the largest goods-producing industry, employment decreased from 13.7 million in December 2007 to 11.5 million in February 2010 and then up by 0.4 million to 11.9 million in February 2012.[15] Manufacturing employment would have to increase by 43.7%, or 5.2 million to return to employment levels in January 2001.

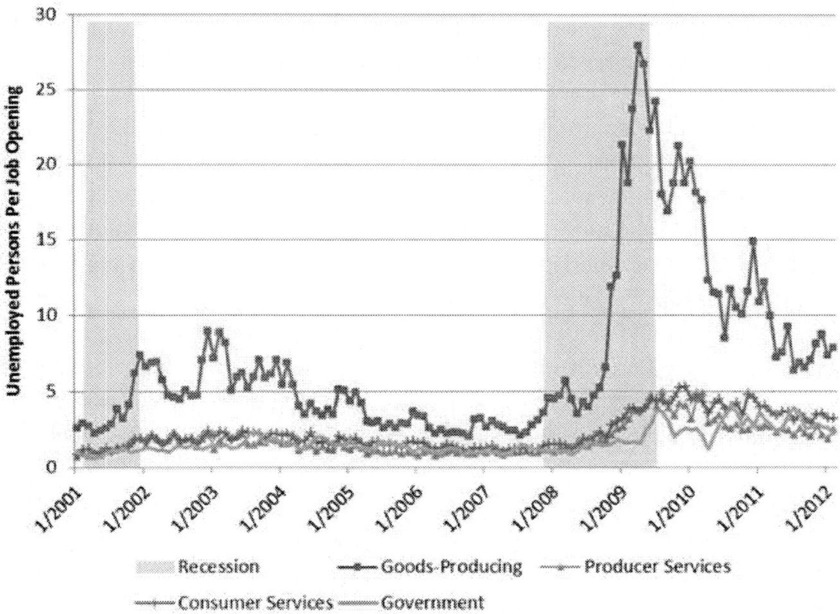

Source: Data on unemployed persons are from the CPS and data on job openings are from the JOLTS.

Notes: Only data that are not adjusted for seasonality are available for unemployment by industry. See Table 1 for information on unemployment and job openings data.

Figure 3. Ratio of Unemployed Persons Per Job Opening Across Industrial Sectors. Monthly Data from January 2001 through February 2012, Not Adjusted for Seasonality.

Fewer jobs in the manufacturing and goods-producing sector as a whole has led to a disproportionate rise in unemployment among male workers. Males, especially the non-college educated, are less likely to be employed in the 2007-2009 recession and previous recessions. The lower employment may relate to disproportionately more persons unemployed from the goods-producing industries like manufacturing and construction. Women on the other hand, have historically been more likely to be employed in less cyclical industries, such as services and public administration.[16]

Knowing that the goods-producing sector has decreased in employment for more than a decade and that the ratio of unemployed persons is consistently higher raises questions about the longterm prospects of the sector and whether policies might make a difference. Whether prospects exist to encourage growth in the manufacturing sector or whether there may be a need to facilitate the transition for unemployed persons in this sector is beyond the scope of this CRS report.

Also, the disproportionate impact of the recession on manufacturing and construction industries raises questions on whether these industries might deserve additional attention during recessionary periods. Even though the ratio for goods-producing jobs has reduced, that may not imply that establishments are hiring all the formerly employed workers. Unemployed workers in these industries may be transitioning to other opportunities.

The ratio of unemployed persons per job opening for consumer services is a relatively low 3.5 in 2011. This sector-wide ratio is lower partly because of lower ratios in the education and health services industry, which is 2.1. The remaining industries had ratios above the sector-wide average ranging between 4.2 and 4.6.

This consumer services sector weathered the recession with a less significant decrease in employment. From December 2007 to February 2012, employment decreased in the consumer services sector by .001 million employees. By comparison, goods-producing employment decreased by 3.7 million.

The Ratio of Unemployed Persons per Job Opening within the Goods-Producing Sector

As shown in the previous section, the ratio of unemployed persons per job opening for the goods-producing sector largely fluctuates with the business cycle in larger proportion to other sectors. To further investigate changes in the ratio over time, each of the goods-producing industries— mining and logging, construction, and manufacturing—are graphed below. A finding in this section is that the ratio for manufacturing and construction rises to very high levels during the 2007-2009 recession.

The ratio of unemployed persons per job opening for goods-producing industries may be of particular interest in that the U.S. Department of Commerce and others suggest that goods-producing industries may provide more benefits relative to other industries. For example, from 2002 through 2011, labor productivity for manufacturing increased more rapidly than aggregate productivity with an average annual increase of 3.4% for manufacturing and 2.3% for all businesses. Since the BLS began publishing hourly earnings, wage growth in the manufacturing industry has kept pace with the private sector increasing by 10.2% in the manufacturing industry and by 10.0% for the private sector. In addition, the Department of Commerce and the National Science Foundation note that the majority of expenditures for Research and Development, 70.1% in 2009, takes place within the manufacturing industry. Note, however, that employment in the manufacturing industry has been decreasing. From 2007 through 2011, total non-farm sector employment decreased by 4.5% in comparison to 15.5% in the manufacturing industry.

Figure 4 shows the ratios of unemployed persons per job opening for the goods-producing industries of mining and logging, construction, and manufacturing. The figure shows that the goods-producing industries are hit hard by the recession.[17] The not seasonally adjusted ratio of unemployed persons per job opening rises to its highest level since the beginning of the data in 2001—66.8 in April 2009 for construction, 31.6 in July 2009 for mining and logging, and 20.7 in May 2009 for manufacturing.[18]

Table A-1 in the Appendix lists the ratios of unemployed persons per job opening for individual industries within the producer services and consumer services for the years 2001 through 2011. The table shows that average monthly ratios of unemployed persons per job opening for the construction and manufacturing sectors are higher for all years, more than twice the other producer and consumer services and government sector. Also, at the high points within the recession, the ratios for the goods-producing industries are more than twice the ratios of the other services-producing industries (12.6 for mining and logging, 34.4 for construction, and 15.8 for manufacturing in comparison to the highest ratio in the services-producing sectors of 6.2 in trade, transportation and utilities).

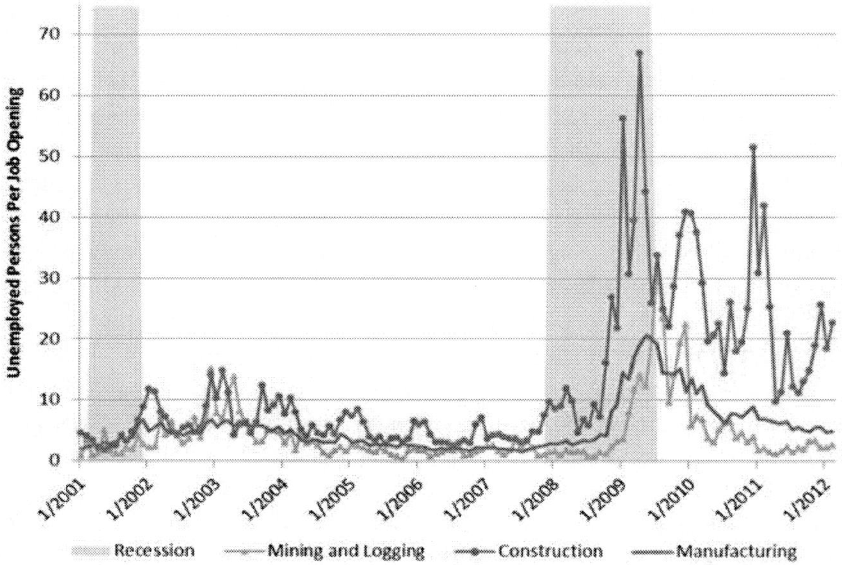

Source: Data on unemployed persons are from the CPS and data on job openings are from the JOLTS.

Notes: Only data that are not adjusted for seasonality are available for unemployment by industry. See Table A-1 for information on unemployment and job openings data.

Figure 4. Unemployed Persons Per Job Opening For Goods-Producing Industries. Monthly Data from January 2001 through February 2012, Not Adjusted for Seasonality.

DISCUSSION

The analysis presented in this report highlights four key findings:

1) The ratio of unemployed persons per job opening is highly correlated with the unemployment rate between 2001 and 2012.
2) The ratio of unemployed persons per job opening rises during the recessionary periods covered in this data set. In the 2007-2009 recession, the ratio rises to very high levels, especially in the goods-producing industries (construction, manufacturing, mining and logging). The higher ratio indicates more unemployed persons for every job opening.

3) Although the ratio is highly correlated with changes in the unemployment rate, the ratio saw modest improvements coming out of the recent recession sooner than the reductions in the unemployment rate. Because job openings was unable to anticipate the high point in unemployment rates after the 2003 recession and because of a limited number of years since the data were first collected (starting in 2001), more years of data would be needed to assess whether and under what circumstances might job openings serve as an early indicator to unemployment.
4) Even though the ratio has reduced, it remains at higher levels than prior to the 2007-2009 recession. Three years after the end of the recession, the ratio still remains higher than any month in the data set prior to the 2007-2009 recession. This may have to do with the depth of the recession and slow job growth since the end of the recession.

A variety of labor market indicators show that the 2007-2009 recession is one of the most severe recessions in the post-World War II era. Unemployment, employment, labor force participation, and hours worked all indicated a substantial deterioration in labor market conditions.[19]

The ratio of unemployed persons per job opening is similar to the unemployment rate with higher ratios during recessions and lower ratios during periods of economic growth, but with some nuanced differences to unemployment rates. For four months following the 2007-2009 recession, unemployment rates continued to climb to 10.0 until October 2009, whereas the ratio of unemployed persons per job opening began to decrease one month after the end of the recession in July 2009. The ratio of unemployed persons per job opening may serve as a useful addition to other labor force statistics providing information on the demand for workers by employers and the population of persons who are currently available for work.

Appendix. Additional Statistics by Industry and Information About the Datasets

This appendix provides data on the ratio of unemployed persons per job opening by industry and year and information about potential limitations of the data.

Table A-1 shows the number of unemployed persons per job opening by industry for each year from 2001 through 2011. The table provides monthly averages for each calendar year and is constructed using data on unemployment from the Current Population Survey (CPS) and data on job openings from the Job Openings and Labor Turnover Survey (JOLTS).

Table A-1. Unemployed Person Per Job Opening By Industry and Year Monthly Averages of Not Seasonally Adjusted Data from 2001 through 2011

Industry	2001	2002	2003	2004	2005	2006	2007	2008	2009	2010	2011
Goods-Producing	3.2	5.7	6.5	4.4	3.3	2.6	2.8	5.4	21.1	12.7	8.2
Mining and Logging	1.7	4.1	5.9	2.3	1.5	1.3	1.7	1.3	12.6	4.5	1.9
Construction	3.5	7.2	7.9	6.0	4.6	3.8	4.3	9.7	34.4	24.7	17.0
Manufacturing	3.2	5.1	5.8	3.7	2.7	2.0	2.1	3.9	15.8	8.7	5.9
Producer Services	1.1	1.8	1.7	1.4	1.0	0.9	1.0	1.5	3.8	3.0	2.4
Information	1.3	3.1	3.4	2.1	1.6	0.8	0.8	2.1	5.6	3.9	2.1
Financial Activities	1.0	1.5	1.6	1.3	0.9	0.8	1.1	1.7	3.9	3.0	2.8
Professional and Business Services	1.1	1.7	1.6	1.3	1.0	1.0	1.0	1.3	3.5	2.9	2.3
Consumer Services	1.2	1.9	2.2	1.9	1.6	1.3	1.3	1.9	4.2	4.2	3.5
Trade, Transportation, and Utilities	1.7	2.8	2.9	2.3	1.9	1.7	1.6	2.6	6.2	5.8	4.3
Education and Health Services	0.6	0.8	1.1	1.0	1.0	0.8	0.8	1.0	2.1	2.4	2.1
Leisure and Hospitality	1.5	2.4	2.6	2.2	1.8	1.5	1.5	2.4	6.0	5.5	4.2
Other Services	1.0	2.1	2.6	2.1	2.0	1.7	1.2	1.8	3.7	3.5	4.6
Government	1.0	1.3	1.7	1.6	1.4	1.1	1.1	1.3	2.4	2.6	3.0
Total	1.4	2.2	2.4	2.0	1.6	1.4	1.4	2.1	5.1	4.5	3.6

Source: Bureau of Labor Statistics, CPS and JOLTS.

Notes: The data are annual averages of the monthly ratio of unemployed persons per job opening, where the monthly ratios are not adjusted for seasonality.

Table A-2 provides additional information about the CPS and JOLTS data that may be useful in understanding the potential limitations of the statistics and analysis.

Table A-2. Description of the Data Used in this Analysis Current Population Survey (CPS) and Job Opening and Labor Turnover Survey (JOLTS)

Category	**Current Population Survey For Estimates on the Number of Unemployed Persons**	**Job Openings and Labor Turnover Survey For Estimates on Job Openings**
Description of the Dataset	The CPS is a survey of households that is designed to represent the civilian noninstitutional population of the United States. Included in the data are information on the labor force and other demographic characteristics.	JOLTS data provide demand-side indicators of labor and labor shortages at the national level. The data include information on job openings, hires quits, layoffs and discharges and involuntary separations.
Statistic Needed for Analysis	Number of Unemployed Persons as a measure of the excess supply of labor	Number of Job Openings as a measure of the demand by employers
Survey Respondents in the Sample	Each month, about 72,000 housing units are assigned for data collection, of which about 60,000 are occupied and thus eligible for interview. Information is obtained each month for about 110,000 persons 16 years of age or older.	The sample is drawn from approximately 8 million establishments in the ES-202 Quarterly Census of Employment and Wages (QCEW) file. This includes private nonagricultural establishments covered under the Unemployment Insurance (UI) system as well as Federal, State, and local government entities in the 50 States and the District of Columbia. Railroads are sampled from an auxiliary frame. The sample does not cover private households or agriculture, forestry, fishing and hunting. However, logging is included.
Are Data Available on a Monthly Basis?	Yes	Yes
Sample Size	Approximately 60,000 households	Approximately 16,000 business establishments

Table A-2. (Continued)

Category	Current Population Survey For Estimates on the Number of Unemployed Persons	Job Openings and Labor Turnover Survey For Estimates on Job Openings
Definition of Statistic Used in the Analysis	Unemployment means not employed during the reference week but were available for work (excluding temporary illness) and had made specific efforts to find employment some time during the four-week period ending with the reference week. Individuals who were waiting to be recalled to a job from which they had been laid off need not have been looking for work to be classified as unemployed. People waiting to start a new job must have actively looked for a job within the last 4 weeks in order to be counted as unemployed. Persons must be at least 16 years old.	A job opening means an employer has a specific position and there is work available for that position. The position can be full-time or part-time, and it can be permanent, short-term, or seasonal. The establishment can start the job within 30 days, whether or not they find a suitable candidate. Also, there is active recruiting for workers from outside the establishment location.
Earliest Date that the Statistic was Available	January 1948	December 2000
Difference in Who, or What, is Included in the Industry Statistics	Unemployment by industry is by last industry the person worked in and excludes new entrants.	Job openings by industry list the number of job openings reported by establishments for each industry. This includes all establishments.
Adjustment for Seasonality (Available Except for Unemployment by Industry)	Unemployment adjusted for seasonality is available for the U.S. and by region, but not by industry.	Job openings adjusted for seasonality is available in the aggregate, by region and by industry.
Differences in When Survey Respondent is Sampled	Persons are asked if they are unemployed during the reference week, which is usually the week including the 12th day of the month.	Establishments are asked to report all job openings on the last business day of the month

Category	Current Population Survey For Estimates on the Number of Unemployed Persons	Job Openings and Labor Turnover Survey For Estimates on Job Openings
Differences in the Most Recently Published Month	Data are published on the first week of the month for data collected during the reference week of the previous month.	Data are published on the second Tuesday or Thursday of each month with preliminary estimates from two months ago and final estimates from three months ago. For example, data published in December include preliminary estimates for October and final estimates for September.
Other Information Available in the Dataset	Unemployment levels by Age, Gender, Race, Education, Occupation and other characteristics are available. Also, the CPS collects information on other labor force statistics such as labor force participation and employment.	Researchers within the BLS are currently working on making data available by establishment size. Other variables besides job openings include employment, job hires, job quits, involuntary separations and other separations from job.
Website for Data	http://www.bls.gov/cps/ht	tp://www.bls.gov/jlt/

Source: CPS website http://www.bls.gov/opub/hom/homch1_itc.htm; and JOLTS website http://www.bls.gov/jlt/.

Table A-3. Aspects of the Data and the Ratio of Unemployed Persons Per Job Opening That May Be Relevant For This Report

Aspects	Description
Difference Between Employment and a Job	A job can be part-time or full-time and temporary or permanent. Also, when a person becomes employed, they may work more than one job.
Adjustment for Seasonality	Data used from both sources are adjusted for seasonality except for unemployment by industry within the CPS. Because of this, the ratio of unemployed persons per job opening is not adjusted for seasonality.

Table A-3. (Continued)

Aspects	Description
Industry Unemployment Statistics	Unemployment by industry includes only those who were formerly employed by an industry and excludes new entrants without previous work experience. The number of persons unemployed in the goods-producing and some other industries may be overstated in that persons who work in central offices are employed in the professional services industry. For example, an employee for an auto manufacturer working in the central office should be classified as working in the professional services industry. Thus some respondents who state the industry they last worked in as manufacturing, goods-producing or some other industry may be misclassified. Analysts from BLS note that efforts are made using other survey responses to minimize such potential errors and suggest that the amounts are small.
When Information is Collected and What is Asked	The differences on when information is collected can produce some differences on the number of unemployed and job openings. Statistics on unemployment are collected during the reference week, which is usually the week that includes the 12th day of the month. Survey respondents are asked if they were unemployed over the last four week period. The number of job openings is for the last business day of the month, which is a shorter period that may not capture as many job openings I comparison to asking over the last four weeks.
Years of Data	The JOLTS data is only available from December 2000 onward, which does not provide any information for recessions in prior years. This maybe particularly relevant in assessing long-term changes such as slowed employment growth dating back 20 years or more.
Who is not Sampled Within JOLTS	The JOLTS data samples from the QCEW and does not include several establishment types such as sole proprietors, religious establishments and agricultural establishments. This might bias some estimates on job openings. For example, sole proprietors who work as contractors in the construction industry may not be included in the job openings statistics.
Aggregate as Opposed to Group Specific	Aggregate statistics with regard to the nation, its four Census regions and industry provide some information, but perhaps more information may be useful with regard to specific groups such as occupations and individual cities.

Aspects	Description
	CPS data provides information on the occupations, place of residence and other demographic statistics. However, JOLTS does not. Employers may have job openings and may be actively recruiting, but may not hire for a longer period of time. Examples of how this may occur is when employers are looking for exact matches to job openings, or when persons are available, but in different geographic locations.
Sample Size	When considering smaller categories, sample sizes may approach smaller amounts, which may reduce the accuracy of the estimates. The CPS roughly samples 60,000 households and the JOLTS roughly samples 16,000 establishments. Even though the samples are weighted to reflect the rest of the population, small subcategories of the data may inherently result in larger variances. This may be especially true if the sub-categories still contain groups that are different in perhaps ways substantively important to understanding the statistic.

Source: Table prepared by the Congressional Research Service (CRS).

End Notes

[1] JOLTS data began one month earlier in December 2000.

[2] The NBER's Business Cycle Dating Committee determines the dates of the recession. In judging when a recession occurs, the committee does not have a fixed set of indicators to define economic activity. It examines various measures: real GDP, economy-wide employment, and real income. The NBER may consider other indicators, such as real sales and the Federal Reserve's index of industrial production. NBER's determination of a recession is different from another common determination often used by the financial press, which is two consecutive quarters of declining real GDP. For more information, see http://www.nber.org/cycles/recessions.html.

[3] The number of unemployed reached a low of 6.7 million in October 2006 and March 2007.

[4] By contrast, the December estimates for the number of unemployed are published in January.

[5] For an example of using the ratio of unemployment per job opening, see Gary L.Podgornik, "Job Openings and Hires Continue to Show Modest Changes in 2011," *Monthly Labor Review*, September 2012, pp. 28-34.

[6] Several caveats must be kept in mind when using the ratio of unemployed person per job opening (listed in detail in the Appendix). Briefly, if persons choose to accept more than one job to any large extent, then the statistic may misrepresent the relative availability of jobs. Second, the ratio may vary across occupations, industries, urban and rural locations, and a variety of other relevant subgroups, which may require more analysis with other data. For example, jobs may be available in other states requiring persons to relocate in order to

take the jobs so that the statistic may not reflect job availability in the short run. As another example, there may be few people to immediately fill a position because the job may require retraining. A third caveat is that even though employers may have job openings, they may be less likely to hire—for example because of more selective screening methods. See Davis, Steven J., R. Jason Faberman, and John C. Haltiwanger, *Recruiting Intensity During and After the Great Recession: National and Industry Evidence*, NBER, Working Paper no. 17782, January 2012, http://www.nber.org/papers/w17782.pdf.

[7] From January 2001 to November 2007, the difference between the unemployment rate (x100, or in percentage points) and the ratio of unemployed persons per job opening ranges from 2.9 to 3.5. The variation in the difference is larger after the 2007-2009 recession, ranging from 2.8 to 5.1. This implies that the unemployment rate tracks more closely with the ratio of unemployed persons per job opening until the recession. This is a comparison between the unemployment rate (scaled by 100) and a ratio, which varies from 0 to infinity.

[8] For data on job hires, see the data retrieval webpage from the BLS JOLTS website, at http://data.bls.gov/pdq/ querytool.jsp?survey=jt.

[9] The aggregate ratio of unemployed persons per job opening is a weighted average off the industrial sectors, where the weights are the share of job openings for the sector to the total number of job openings. Because of this, an increase in the ratio for one sector will result in an increase in the aggregate ratio of unemployed persons per job opening.

[10] Producer services are classified using the following citations, where an issue commonly addressed is where to classify the trade, transportation, and utilities. Most of the studies do not include trade, transportation, or utilities as producer services. However, some studies include utilities as goods-producing industries. Because the BLS groups these industries together and because trade and transportation make up the majority of employment, the industry is categorized as a consumer service. For articles classifying producer services, see C. Michael Wernerheim and Christopher A. Sharpe, "Producer services and the 'mixed-market' problem: some empirical evidence," *Area*, vol. 31, no. 2 (1999), pp. 123-140. Daniel P. Lindahl and William B. Beyers, "The Creation of Competitive Advantage by Producer Service Establishments," Economic Geography, vol. 73, no. 1 (January 1999), pp. 1-20. James R. Markusen, "Trade in Producer Services and in Other Specialized Intermediate Inputs," The American Economic Review, vol. 79, no. 1 (March 1989), pp. 85-95.

[11] If the ratio of unemployed persons per job opening is larger in one sector compared with another, then the share of unemployed persons divided by the share of job openings for the sector will also be larger. This is because the ratio of unemployed persons per job opening times a constant equals the ratio of the shares, where the constant is the same across all industries.

[12] Because BLS does not produce seasonally adjusted data for unemployment or job openings by industry or sector, the ratios constructed for the figure are also unadjusted for seasonality.

[13] These numbers correspond to the beginning of the recession in December 2007 to the lowest level of employment— October 2009 for producer services and January 2010 for consumer services. The decreased employment corresponds to an increased number of unemployed persons who worked in each of these industries. During the same months, unemployment rises by 1.6 million in goods-producing, 1.4 million in producer services, and 1.9 million in consumer services sectors.

[14] For example, higher housing prices might have temporarily prevented declines in employment in the manufacturing industry. See Kerwin Ko Charles, Erik Hurst, and Matthew J. Notowidigdo, *Manufacturing Busts, Housing Booms, and Declining Employment: A*

Structural Explanation, Federal Reserve Bank of Atlanta, papers presented at the conference on Employment Consequences of the Great Recession, Atlanta, GA, September 14, 2012, http://www.frbatlanta.org/documents/news/conferences/12employment_charles_hurst_noto.pdf. See also CRS Report R41898, *Job Creation in the Manufacturing Revival*, by Marc Levinson.

[15] Data are seasonally adjusted and from the Current Employment Survey maintained by the Bureau of Labor Statistics: http://data.bls.gov/pdq/querytool.jsp?survey=ce.

[16] See Hilary W.Hoynes, Douglas L. Miller, and Jessamyn Schaller, *Who Suffers During Recessions?*, NBER, Working Paper no. 17951, March 2012, http://www.nber.org/papers/w17951, and Kerwin Ko Charles, Erik Hurst, and Matthew J. Notowidigdo, "Manufacturing Busts, Housing Booms, and Declining Employment: A Structural Explanation," Federal Reserve Bank of Atlanta, papers presented at the conference on Employment Consequences of the Great Recession, Atlanta, GA, September 14, 2012, http://www.frbatlanta.org/documents/news/conferences/12employment_charles_hurst_noto.pdf.

[17] During the 137 months since the beginning of the dataset (2001), the ratio of unemployed persons per job opening is higher than the services industry or government sector for every month except two for the construction industry and for 10 months for the manufacturing industry.

[18] As precautionary notes, JOLTS data do not include sole proprietors (or individual contractors), which may inflate the ratios depending on how many households hire sole proprietors. In addition, the height of these peaks may partly reflect the seasonality of the data, but even when averaging the monthly information into years. in the **Appendix** shows that the peak of the ratios in 2009 for mining and logging (12.6), construction (34.4) and manufacturing (15.8) are more than twice that of the other industries.

[19] Michael W. Elsby, Bart Hobijn, and Aysegul Sahin, *The Labor Market in the Great Recession*, NBER, Working Paper no. 15979, May 2010, http://www.nber.org/papers/w15979.

INDEX

D

E

F

G

H

I

J

L

M

N

O

P

V

W

Y